PROFITABILITY TRENDS AND BUSINESS CYCLES

Profitability Trends and Business Cycles

A Comparative Study of Manufacturing Sectors of U.K. and India

Dr. (Mrs.) Lata Arun Rede
Professor of Economics (D.S.A.)

Department of Economics
Faculty of Arts
M. S. University of Baroda

1998

DISCOVERY PUBLISHING HOUSE
NEW DELHI—110 002

Published by :

Discovery Publishing House
4831/24, Ansari Road, Prahlad Street
Darya Ganj, New Delhi—110 002 (INDIA)
Phone : 327 92 45
Fax : 91–11–3253475

First Published—1998

ISBN 81–7141–413–3

Laser Typeset by :

Allied Computers,
Karnal (Haryana)

Printed at :

Tarun Offset Printers
Delhi-53

Preface

Profitability of a firm measures its financial viability on one hand, and also plays a pivotal role in the growth process of the concern, the industry, and the economy. The movement of capital from non-profitable to profitable fields is very crucial to the efficiency and growth of the industry and the economy. Profitability of a concern reflects its financial stability and also enhances its earning capacity. It plays dual role in the investment process of the industry and the economy by attracting new investment and providing internal source of finance. Various groups of people are interested in knowing the profitability of a concern or an industry for various purposes like investment, lending, taxation, or purely academic interests.

Inspite of significant role played by rate of profit in the investment and growth process of the industry and the economy, it has remained a neglected area of research.

The recent events of breakup of erstwhile U.S.S.R., and, union of East and West Germany, under the great influence of the global wave of privatisation, evoked us to enquire into the profitability trends and business cycles in two different types of economies, viz., a developing mixed economy like India, and, a developed capitalist economy like U.K. Thus, the influence of the wave of privatisation across all economic, social, political ideologies, tempted us to initiate the efforts in the comparative study of profitability trends and business cycles in manufacturing sectors of India and U.K. The attempt of more than 50 countries of the world towards opening up of competition, both for domestic and world markets, beyond doubt, expresses peoples' strong faith in the sanctity of private property, and, freedom of choice to all economic units. This has re-enforced their unshaken belief in the efficient working of competitive market economy, which is based on price-profit mechanism.

Though there have been a few separate studies undertaken on profitability and related issues like size, growth, concentration, etc. in countries like U.S.A., U.K., India, etc., a comparative study on profitability trends and business cycles in manufacturing sectors of two different types of economies, e.g., a developing mixed economy like India, and a developed capitalist economy like U.K., is completely missing. This study makes an attempt to fill up the gap.

It is a widely accepted fact that business cycles are found to be an ever present force in market economies based on free enterprise system. Hence, the knowledge about the presence of business cycles would help the concern to minimize losses or maximize profits. Considering all these matters, an attempt is made in the present study to examine the profitability trends of 19 Indian and 17 U.K. manufacturing Industries over the period 1960–61 to 1988–89, i.e., 29 years. Moreover, based on these rates of profit, an attempt is made to explore the existence of phases of contraction and expansion, turning points like trough and peaks, and amplitude and periodicity of business cycles in these two countries, and, the results derived are then compared. We are sure, that, the study will be of interest to all those who wish to understand well the economics of industrial activity in two different types of economies. The study combines empirical data with historical facts in order to see the effect of the government policy. However, this being more or less a preliminary attempt, its results may be treated as experimental. The author craves indulgence for errors in proof corrections caused due to hectic pace.

The present study was undertaken and completed during one year Sabbatical Leave (from 1st October 1993 to 30th September, 1994) granted for undertaking this post-doctoral research project. I take this opportunity of expressing a deep sense of gratitude towards, the M.S. University authorities for granting me the sabbatical leave.

I am deeply indebted to U.G.C., for providing me financial aid in order to collect data and source material from U.K. via a short visit of 4 weeks to U.K. in March–April, 1990.

I take this opportunity to express my gratitude towards British High Commission for expediting my visa and immigration formalities, alongwith arranging my meetings with experts in U.K. This has helped my project a long way. I do not find adequate words to express deep sense of gratitude towards Professor I.G. Patel, Ex-Director, and Professor Meghnad Desai, London School of Economics and Political Science, London, U.K. I am greatly thankful to the Librarian, British Library of Political and Economic Science, London School of Economics and Political Science, London; Librarian, Cambridge University Library, U.K.; and Librarian, The British Council Library, New Delhi, for providing me library facilities and supplying required, information, reading material and data on British manufacturing sector.

I wish to acknowledge with gratitude the Librarian, Reserve Bank of India (R.B.I.); Mr. K.S. Rao, Assistant Adviser, Department of Statistical Analysis and Computer Services, R.B.I., for supplying me the computer print outs of Financial Statements of Indian Manufacturing Industries for the period 1981–82 to 1988–89, as these were not separately published by R.B.I.

Prof. M.M. Dadi, Dean, Faculty of Management Studies, M.S. University, Baroda, who was also my Ph.D. Supervisor, has been a constant source of inspiration, valuable suggestions and encouragement till the completion of this study. I cannot find adequate words to express my deep sense of gratitude to my revered Professor for encouraging me and showing keen interest in undertaking and completing the arduous task of this project.

I wish to express my gratitude to the sources wherefrom I have borrowed profoundly the data and the matters for this work.

I wish to express my deep sense of gratitude to my friends,

colleagues and all those who have assisted me in any form in the completion of this work.

I am thankful to Mr. B.C. Patel for providing data processing support through statistical packages on Computer for my project.

I am very thankful to Mr. Isaac N., I.C.S.S.R. Fellow, working under my supervision for Ph.D. for all type of support and help in getting data, reading, and, source material for the project. I am thankful to Mr. C.N. Kachhia for seeing manuscript through the final stage of typing with utmost care without delay.

Last, but not least, I shall be failing in my duty if I did not acknowledge with gratitude the strenuous work put in by my son, Mr. Sandeep A. Rede, till the completion of this study, and, full cooperation extended by my daughter, and daughter-in-law.

Dr. (Mrs.) Lata Arun Rede

Contents

1
Introduction

Significance of the Study

The period of 1980's has witnessed worldwide phenomenon of privatisation, which has caused revolution in economic philosophy of various countries of the world. The global wave of privatisation, initiated by U.K. during Margaret Thatcher's regime, significantly influenced all types of economic, social and political ideologies and succeeded greatly in carrying the message of efficient working of price-profit mechanism under competitive, capitalist form of economic system. Consequently, the world witnessed the breakdown of communist ideologies and breaking up of erstwhile U.S.S.R., and, the Union of East and West Germany in early 1990's.

This entire transformation, beyond doubt, expresses peoples' strong faith in the sanctity of private property, freedom of choice as consumers, workers, investors, producers, etc., and their unshaken belief in the efficient working of market mechanism. Obviously, profitability, a fulcrum around which the entire business activity rotates has started gaining back its place which it held in classical theories.

Profitability of various industries would hardly diverge in a world of perfection, because, future can easily be predicted. However, real world is far from perfection. A number of dynamic forces (e.g., changes in income, technology, population, etc.) operate simultaneously in a real imperfect and uncertain world. Consequently, profitability of different concerns and industries gets greatly affected.

Rate of profit which is one of the most used and popular financial measure of performance of a concern and an industry, plays a pivotal role in the growth process of the concern, the industry and the whole economy. It reflects the financial stability and also enhances the earning capacity of the concern. It plays dual role in the investment process of the economy by attracting fresh investment on one hand, and, generating internal source of finance on the other hand. However, low rate of profit or loss repels any fresh inflow of investment and induces existing capital to quit towards the fields of higher rates of profit. It thus reflects investors' and lenders' need of knowing financial indicator of performance and is a key factor in determining the commercial viability of the concern and the industry.

In developed capitalist countries like U.K. a wide-spread dissatisfaction with additional cost-accounting systems has recently been expressed in corporate sector as these have failed to capture the essence of new manufacturing environment (Bhimani, 1, 1993). The use of non-financial measures of performance is strongly advocated for manufacturing industries which have adopted advanced technologies and redesigned work processes. It is argued that novel non-financial performance measures are needed to capture and emerging emphasis on quality, just-in-time delivery and increasing product ranges etc. Financial measures of performance are hardly of any use for the control of production or distribution. The factory operators bother for production rates, yield quantities, reject rates, schedule changes, stock-outs, on time delivery, quality of design, etc., which can be expressed better by non-financial indicators. Hence, it is sometimes advocated that financial and non-financial performance measures be combined in a complementary way so that both parties, the internal ones like managers and executives and the external parties like bankers, financiers, investors, government etc., receive accurate and comprehensive information needed to measure the performance of a concern.

However, on the basis of a study conducted for 21 U.K. manufacturing companies, Dr. Bhimani (2, 1994) concludes that though performance measures vary according to condition, most companies have a tendency to follow financial performance indicators. Moreover, investors, lenders, bankers, board members, etc. overwhelmingly rely on financial measures like profit, return on capital, turnover, cash flow etc. In other words, variety of financial and non-financial performance measures, constitute an important element of decision-making, and need to be appropriately used by manufacturing sector. However considering the differences in the adoption and availability of technologies and information systems in India and U.K., the present study has opted to rely on most popular financial measure of performance of an industry, viz., Rate of Profit.

Objective

Though a number of experts have separately examined the profitability and related issues like size, growth, concentration in manufacturing sectors of various countries like U.S.A. (Epstein, 28, 1934; Stigler 98, 1963), U.K. (Hart, P.E., 39, 1965, 1968; Singh A. and Whittington, G., 95, 1968). India (Mehta, 57, 1961; Rede, 78, 79 and 81, 1983, 1984, 1988) etc., a comparative study of profitability of a developed capitalist country, and a developing country's manufacturing industries is essentially lacking. Moreover, inspite of the inherent tendency of competitive economic systems to become subject to business cycles or economic fluctuations, a comparative study of profitability trends and business cycles in manufacturing sectors of various countries is completely missing. The present study proposes to fill up the lacuna.

Manufacturing sectors of U.K. and India are operating under different economic, political, technological, organizational, etc., environments. India resorted to planned economic growth through speedy industrialisation after she acquired freedom. The tempo of industrialisation picked up since the launching of second Five Year Plan in 1955-66. Mahalanobis strategy of speedy regulation of private sector was adopted. Since then India has been passing through vigorous and qualitative industrial transformation. The adoption of mixed economy gave recognition to the coexistence of public and private sectors.

On the other hand side, U.K. a capitalist developed country, has well-developed industrial sector with relatively less government intervention in industrial sector. The study of profitability trends and business cycles is to be undertaken, considering the different industrial environments and stages of industrial development in these two countries.

The current rate of profit is an indicator and source of and a need for the expansion of a business through reinvestment and through attracting and absorbing new capital in the industry. Hence, investors and lenders are interested in knowing the profitability of a concern and industry over time or at a point of time. Since profits provide a good source of revenue to the government, its knowledge is useful while framing the taxation policy. Economists and other academicians are interested in empirical testing of various hypothesis forwarded regarding rate of profit and thus provide guidelines to the government in framing economic policies. In short, the word profit attracts various groups of people like businessmen, accountants, tax collectors, workers, economists, investors, lenders etc. Obviously, study of profitability has attracted our attention due to its various practical uses, and due to complete absence of comparative study of profitability of manufacturing sectors of developed and developing countries. This has induced us further to pursue this study so that the gap in the area is filled up.

Issues Explored

Since the present study aims at comparative analysis of profitability trends and business cycles in manufacturing sectors of U.K. and India, we have relied upon the concept of profit rate which is followed for U.K. industries and have attempted to explore the following issues. The period covered is 1960–61 to 1988–89, i.e., 29 years.

(A) Profitability Trends

The celebrated tendency of rates of profit to fall over a

long period of time had been theoretically developed by classical economists like Adam Smith, David Ricardo, etc., their critic Karl Marx and also by neoclassical writers like Alfred Marshall. The study therefore intends to empirically examine whether the rates of profit in Indian and U.K. Manufacturing industries have a tendency to rise or fall over a fairly long period of 29 years. The objective here is not to test the validity of classical hypothesis as the economic conditions as assumed by classical writers do not prevail in both these countries. However, a knowledge about whether profitability is rising or falling over the period 1960-61 to 1988-89 would throw interesting results for formulation of future policies.

(B) Profitability Trends and Business Cycles

The cyclical fluctuations, or, alternating period of prosperity and depression, are found to be an ever present force in market economies based on free enterprise system. The knowledge about the presence of these fluctuations and the surrounding economic conditions, may help the concern to avoid losses and to avail chances of making profit, as much as possible. Though business cycles exert tremendous influence on the rate of return and the stock of capital of various concerns, it has remained a relatively neglected area of research, especially, as far as comparative study of various countries is concerned. Hence, the present study has made an attempt to examine the influence of business cycles on the profitability ratios of various British and Indian manufacturing industries over the period 1960-61 and 1988-89. To what extent do business cycles influence profitability of these industries? What is the duration of an average peak-through-peak cycle in British and Indian industries? which industries are liable to more fluctuations in these countries? How many phases of expansion and contraction are experienced by these industries? These and the related issues are resolved in this section.

Sources and Coverage of Data

For examining the various aspects of profitability mentioned above, the study has relied upon the following sources of data for India and U.K.

(A) For India

The study is based on the series of combined accounts (Balance Sheets. Income Statements, etc.) of different industries published by Reserve Bank of India (RBI) in its publication on "Financial Statistics of Joint Stock Companies in India (1967.1975) in two volumes and in various issues of R.B.I. Bulletins. For the period 1981–82 to 1988–89, the study has relied upon the computer printouts of combined accounts of the same industries provided by Department of Company Finance, R.B.I. on our request. and, the author is highly indebted to them for their co-operation. Only large and medium public limited companies are covered for the period 1960–61 to 1988–89. Companies with paid up capital of Rs. 0.5 million or more are covered in this study. Nineteen manufacturing industries out of Thirty-one, for which data are available for the study period (1960–61) in 1988–89) are selected.

The number of companies covered by these 19 industries has been gradually increasing, and, data are revised every five years since 1960–61. Since the objective of this study is to examine the profitability ratio of whole industry, we have attempted to incorporate as many companies in an industry as possible. Thus, the number of companies has increased from 754 (56.6%) in 1960–61 to 921 (61.4%) in 1965–66, 1068 (64.4%) in 1970–71 and 1058 (68.5%) in 1975–76, 1053 (61.2%) in 1980–81 and 1117 (63.4%) in 1985–86[1].

Most of the companies covered in earlier series have been covered in latter series also. Most of the companies which went into production during the five-year period preceding the commencement of the latter series were included in it.

The coverage has been kept around 80% in terms of paid-up capital of all the non-governmental, non-financial public limited companies, at the commencement of the each of the series, without bothering for the difference in the numbers of

1 Figures in brackets indicate the percentage of companies covered in this study out of the total number of companies covered in this subsector in R.B.I. sample, i.e., out of 1333 companies in 1960–61, 1501 in 1965–66, 1650 in 1970–71 and 1720 in 1975–76 and 1980–81..and 1763 in 1985–86.

public limited companies covered. Companies with paid-up capital of Rs. 0.5 million each or above (estimated at historical costs) are classified as medium or large companies.

Amongst the studies on the finances of the cooperates sector of India, the R.B.I. studies on medium and large public limited companies are the most important ones and cover a substantially long period. The distribution of companies according to the size of the paid up capital is found to be highly skew. In 1964-65, the companies having paidup capital above Rs.0.5 million or more accounted for over 95% of the total paidup capital of all non-governmental, non-financial public limited companies. However, in terms of number of companies, these formed only 38% of total number of companies in corporate sector. The large coverage in terms of paid up capital was the main aspect which induced us to study only a limited number of companies with paidup capital of Rs. 0.5 million or above. Moreover, the R.B.I. sample of 1333 companies (38% of total) in 1964-65 implied that there were around 3508 companies in the whole sub-sector. The present study covers 754 of these companies, i.e., 21.5% of the total number of companies with around 55% of paidup capital in this sub-sector. Hence, it is considered to be a good representative of the whole sector, and hence, has been chosen for the study.

The role played by manufacturing sector in Indian economy is reflected via it's increasing share in net domestic product which stood around 13.9% in 1960-61 and 15.6% in 1977-78, and 19.7% in 1988-89.

Since the R.B.I. studies provide data on profitability ratios and the related concepts based on financial statements, it was preferred over the data published by Annual Survey of Industry (ASI), though the latter covered wider all India manufacturing field. Moreover, data on profitability ratios and related concepts are easily obtainable on continuous and comparable basis for a fairly long period from R.B.I. studies. Finally, the R.B.I. data provides a good sample for the manufacturing sector of India. Hence, the study heavily relied upon the R.B.I. published data on company finances.

The study for Indian Manufacturing sector is based on the

R.B.I. Classification of Industries, which divides industries on the basis of main line of activity.

(B) For U.K.

The data for British manufacturing industries are based on the series of combined accounts (Balance Sheets, Income and Appropriation Accounts) of manufacturing industries in various issues of Business Monitor, Company Finance (41), published by H.M.S.O., London, U.K. The data covers listed companies. The companies whose securities have been admitted to the official list of the Stock Exchange are termed as listed companies. All types of listed companies, small, medium and large are covered[2]. The criteria for selection of the panel of companies from which the analysis is derived have changed over the years. Companies with net assets of £0.5 million or more or gross income of £50,000 or more were covered in 1960. There was a change in this coverage in 1968 because of which companies with net assets of £2.0 million or more, or gross income of £200,000 or more were included. This has reduced the coverage by 1½ per cent in terms of average net assets (for both listed and unlisted companies). This was partly because private companies could no longer be exempt from producing accounts and the analysis of unlisted companies as a result included some large companies which were previously private exempt. The effect of this change within some of the industry groups was more marked. The latest criterion relates, to companies with net assets of £5.0 million or more, or gross income of £500,000 or more for listed companies for 1976, produced a panel of 1626 companies of which 1129 were listed and 497 unlisted.

The listed companies for 1977-78 accounted for 84% of total net assets of all companies in manufacturing and distribution. Great Britain subsidiaries of parent companies registered in North Ireland or Overseas and the subsidiaries of the National Enterprise Board are also included. Around 3000 companies are covered by end of the study. Thus, the number

2. Small companies have capital employed upto £ 1 million Medium companies have capital employed between £1 to £4.16 million, and Large Companies had capital employed above £ 4.16 million.

of companies covered kept on increasing.

Standard industrial clarification of 1968 and 1980 upto two or three digists for manufacturing industries is adopted. Industries are classified according to their main activity, and hence, the combined data for industries would include figures relating to the subsidiary activities including in that group.

Business Monitor provides data on old series which covers the period 1960-61 to 1976-77 and new series from 1977-78 onwards. The accounts of a fully representative sample of Great Britain industrial and commercial companies, independent company or company groups has been undertaken by Business Monitor so that comparable series from 1977-78 could be provided. The figures provided by Business Monitor are based on the consolidated annual accounts of independent companies, or, company groups engaged mainly in the U.K. in manufacturing, distribution, construction, transport, property and certain other services. The present study relates only to those industries which belong to manufacturing sector and cover the period 1960-61 to 1988-89.

It is essential to point out here that there is a vast difference in the level and stages of economic and industrial development of U.K. and India. A few statistics are provided to confirm this. GNP (Gross National Product) per capita in U.S. dollars for U.K. was estimated to be 12810 in 1988 while for India it was around 340 in same year. As regards annual rate of growth of GNP between 1965-1988, both the countries had it at 1.8 per cent; however, the GNP for U.K. was 37.7 times greater than for India.

Similarly, share of Industrial Sector in real GDP stood around 4.2% for U.K. in 1978 and 19.7% for India in 1975, while manufacturing sector 28.7%, to real GDP in U.K. in 1978, and 8.5% in 1975 for India. These statistics clearly depict the relative positions of these two economies by end of 1970's.

Methodology

The present study applies a number of statistical tools like mean, standard deviation, coefficient of variation etc., to examine the relative and absolute dispersion in profitability ratios of Indian and British manufacturing industries over the study period. This enables us to capture inter-industry and industry wise variations in profit rates.

Profitability trends are estimated by estimating time trend coefficients for each of these industries over the study period. The statistical technique of regression is applied to deprive the results. The industries are classified into five major sectors, viz., Consumers goods, basic goods, capital, goods, intermediary goods and the whole manufacturing sector. This classification is based on the guidelines provided by R.B.I. classification.

On the basis of the results derived through profitability trends for each industry in these countries, an attempt is made to detect business cycles, which would still be prevalent in the series. The most commonly used method of separating trend and business cycles in a series is to express the actual data for profit rate as a percentage of trend value for each year. The business cycle thus located are termed deviation cycles. Another method is to compare the rate of growth of actual profit rate to that of its trend value. These are termed as growth cycles. The present study makes an attempt to detect deviation cycles in the profit rates of Indian and British manufacturing industries.

Limitations of the Study

A comparative study of profitability trends and business cycles, based on combined accounts of joint stock or listed companies of India and U.K. suffers from following limitations.

1) Firstly, the concept of profit rate adopted in this study is financial one and hence price variations are not taken into account.

2) Secondly, the study is based on the profit rate which measures profitability on long term capital. Due to limited period of 4 weeks' visit to U.K., the author could obtain the profitability ratios of U.K. manufacturing industries as were published in Business Monitor, Company Fi-

nance. For comparability purposes, therefore, series on profitability of Indian Manufacturing industries were to be prepared in accordance with that available for British Industries. Profits are defined not of depreciation and interest on short term loans, and capital consists of net fixed inflation, fixed assets tent to be undervalued in company accounts and causes under statement of denominator of the profitability ratio. However, profits, the numerator of the profit rate, gets overstated due to very low depreciation charges.

3) Thirdly, companies give information on loans existing at the end of one year. Therefore, loans rapid/written-off within a short period of 3-4 months do not enter the final figures whereas companies invariably give the full amount of interest charges as a total lost of loans (i.e., existing plus written-off loans). Therefore, inclusion of interest charges in profits leads to overstating of profit rates if there exist some loans which are written off.

4) Since R.B.I. and Business Monitor data for India and U.K. respectively are based on the documents like annual reports and accounts of the selected companies, there are subject to following limitations.

The statements on Balance Sheets, Income and Expenditure Accounts, etc., show only the combined position and not the consolidated one for the group of companies for which the data are presented, because, the inter-corporate transactions are not eliminated while combining the data.

5) The companies are grouped according to the main activity, hence, combined data for a particular industry would include figures relating to the subsidiary activities included in that group. Studies relating to industries are, however, bound to suffer from this sort of limitation, irrespective of the source of data.

The Indian data provided by the Department of Company Affairs on paid-up capital is used to arrive at coverage of paid-up capital in each industrial group. The

Industrial Classification of the Department is based on the objectives set out in the memorandum of Association filled at the time of registration of the company, whereas, the main line of activity, as revealed by the annual reports and accounts of the Company forms the basis of classification of the Industry in R.B.I. studies. However, the present study is not affected much by this limitation. As regards U.K., the division of companies in industry according to their main activity sometimes covers out of scope and overseas activities too.

6) A macro level comparative study of this type suffers from the fact that certain influences different industries in same country in different ways as these work under different conditions. The difference are further widened in different countries, especially if these are economically very different. However, there is no escape from this limitation.

Moreover, age components of different industries in a country differ greatly, obviously, for different countries the variations would be very high. For example, cotton and Jute Textile industries are nearly 140 years old in India while medicines and Pharmaceutical industry and majority of capital goods industries are hardly 50-52 years old. Between India and U.K., these differences are much more wider as industrialisation in U.K. started in 18th century while it began in India almost in mid-twentieth century. However, a comparative macro level study has to bear with these limitation and the conclusions need to be derived accordingly.

8) Besides measurement problems, there are other difficulties in using profitability as a measure of performance. Jones and Cockerill (47, 1987, p. 80) argue that high rates of profits may be the result of monopoly power in the product market enabling the firm to charge a price greater than marginal cost through the absence of competitors. Similarly, a monopronist firm may succeed in obtaining the inputs at prices below the competitive markets.

Similarly, a fall in the profit rate may be the outcome of entry of new firms into the market, reducing the overall rate of profit, but, improving the performance of the industry, and it may also be indicative of rise in costs of the first or reduction in competitiveness in the industry.

Inspite of all these limitations the data for both U.K. and Indian manufacturing industries constitute the core of statistical infrastructure in the field of industrial finance and enable the undertaking of a comparative study of their manufacturing sectors and hence, the study has heavily relied on these sources.

2

Rate of Profit : Concept and Measurement

Introduction

Profitability is a ratio derived from two terms, viz., Profits and Capital. However, these two concepts themselves are highly controversial. Since profits are looked at differently by different groups of people e.g., investors, entrepreneurs, tax-collectors, etc., the choice of the term profits depends upon the purpose of inquiry. Moreover, the profits need to be related to capital so that profit rate is derived. Obviously, the concept of capital chosen has to correspond well to the concept of profits taken. This leaves us with a number of concepts of profit rates used in business practices and in research studies like (a) gross profits[1] as percentage of total capital employed[2], (b) net profits (net of interest charges, provision of tax and depreciation) as percentage of net worth (includes paid-up capital premium on capital and all reserves except depreciation and taxation reserves) (c) Profits before tax (gross of interest charges on long term borrowings and net of interest charges on short term borrowings) as percentage of long term capital employed (which

1. Gross Profits include interest charges, provision for taxation, dividends and retained profits. These may be inclusive or exclusive of depreciation charges, as the need may be.

2. Capital Employed include total assets which equal total liabilities and may be taken net or gross of depreciation charges as the case may be.

includes fixed assets plus current assets minus current liabilities), etc. As regards depreciation charges, these are to be either included in both, the profits and capital, or, to be excluded from the both, as per the purpose of the inquiry.

The concept of profitability defined in (a) above is termed as gross profit rate and is an indicator of the efficiency of employing all the capital for earning profits. It thus provides the return on investment concept which is derived from the product of two other ratios, *viz.*, "Profit margin" (Profits + Sales) and "turnover ratio of Capital" (Sales divided by total capital employed).

Concept (b), net profit rate, is an indicator of the efficiency with which shareholders' equity capital is used to earn profit' in the industry. It gives guidelines to the investors and deals with only equity capital, leaving the characteristics of borrowed capital unexplained.

The third concept, (c), explained above provides an idea about the efficiency with which long term capital (equity plus long term borrowed capital or funded capital) is used to earn profits in the industry. This is considered to be a better measure of industry's earning power, if the purpose is to analyse the performance of the industry over a long period of time. Moreover, this has been found to be a most common definition used in comparing corporate industrial performance[3] in most of the countries.

It is obvious from above mentioned variety of definitions of profit rate that the choice of its definition depends upon the purpose of inquiry, implying thereby that there is no inherent sanctity in the choice of this ratio. Since the present study relates to comparative analysis of profitability of Indian and British manufacturing industries over a fairly long period of twenty nine years (1960-61 to 1988-89), we had to choose that concept of profitability which helped in measuring long term profitability of various industries. Moreover, the data on profit

3. The concept of long term profit rate has been followed in U.K. by Monopolies Commission, Business Monitor, Company Finance, H.M.S.O., London, and experts like Singh, A. and Whittington, G. (96, 1968) and by ESRF (24, 1964) in India.

rates for British manufacturing sector were collected by the author during her short visit or four weeks to U.K. Hence, we had to rely upon the profit rate data which were easily and readily available from Business Monitor, Company Finance, H.M.S.O., London, U.K., and which were obtained by the author from the Library of London School of Politics and Economics. The data for Indian Manufacturing industries were gathered from R.B.I. publications on Company Finances of Joint Stock Companies in India. The period covered is 1960-61 to 1988-89 for the both countries. This study thus defines profits and capital employed in the following manner.

Profits Defined In This Study

(A) For U.K. Manufacturing Industries

Profits are taken net of depreciation and are termed as net income for U.K. industries. Net income (profits) is derived by deducting depreciation from gross income. The latter includes trading profits and other income, depreciation and other prior year adjustments other than tax. The trading profits are derived by deducting manufacturing expresses from the income from sales of the product, and exclude directors' fees and emoluments, pensions to past directors, super annuation payments, compensation for loss of office, auditors fees, etc. To the trading profits is added other income which includes income from trade investments, other investments and sources.

In other words, net income or profits for U.K. manufacturing industries are derived from the summation of interest on long term borrowings or funded capital, taxation, dividends and retained profits. Thus these are net of depreciation charges and interest on short term borrowings. These profits therefore show the returns accruing to long term capital employed.

(B) For Indian Manufacturing Industries

As regards India, the author in her publication (Rede, 79, 1984) had followed two different concepts of profitability for Indian manufacturing industries, viz., gross profits (which include interest on short and long term loans, taxation, dividends and retained profits) and net profits (which include only dividends and retained profits), covering the period 1950-51 to 1977-78. However, to have the comparative analysis, she has to modify the concept of profits according to what is adopted for U.K. industries. This required lot of exercise due to nonavailability of the type of data required. Following method was therefore adopted to prepare comparable series of profits for Indian Manufacturing industries covering the period 1960-61 to 1988-89.

The R.B.I. data on Financial Statistics of Joint Stock Companies in India, provide industry-wise data on Profit/loss accounts wherein gross profit (derived after deducting manufacturing expenses and depreciation from total income) comprise of interest on short and long term borrowings, provision for taxation, dividends and retained profits. Thus, the accounts do not provide separate data on interest on short term and long term borrowings. In order to make the profits concept comparable with that followed for U.K., it was necessary to estimate interest charges on short term borrowings and to deduct these from gross profits.

Since data on interest on short term borrowings could not directly be obtained from published figures, we had to rely upon our own estimates from the available data. Imputation of interest on short term loans via application of interest rate would have required choice of definite interest rate to be applied. However rate of interest differs according to the term of borrowing and the type of industry, etc. Since different industries borrows funds for different time periods, it was not possible to get full details on breakup of interest charges. Choosing average rate of interest would have involved lot of exercise and arbitration. Hence, the only way left to us was to rely upon the information available on the breakup of total borrowings into short term and long term borrowings. This gave us an idea about proportion of short term or long term borrowings in total borrowings. On the basis of this information we estimated the ratios of short term borrowings to total borrowings for each industry over the study period. In order to estimate interest charges on short term borrowings, we applied these ratio to the total interest charges. The amount thus estimated as then deducted (as interest charges on short borrowings) from total interest so that interest on the long term borrowings could be obtained. This exercise had an implied assumption that proportion of short term interest charges in total interest charges equaled that of proportion of short term borrowings in total borrowings for each industry and for each year. In the absence of any other detailed information of the breakup of interest charges on short and long term borrowings we had to resort to this less objectionable methods of estimating interest charges on short and long term borrowings. This exercise was carried out for each industry over the entire study period.

After obtaining the series of interest charges on short term borrowings for each industry for the study period, these were deducted from total interest charges for each industry for each year, thus leaving us with the respective series of interest on long term capital. This enabled us to prepare to comparable series of Profits for each Indian manufacturing industry for the study period. Hence, Profits estimated for these industries, comprise of interest on long term borrowings, provision for taxation, dividends and retained profits.

In short, profits defined for Indian manufacturing industries are derived after deducting from total income, the manufacturing expenses, depreciation, and interest on short term loans, and, include long term interest accruing to long term capital employed, i.e., equity and long term borrowings.

Both the series of profits for U.K. and India include other income or non-operating income which accrues due to activities other than the sales of output. It includes interest and dividends earned on the outside investment and administrative income such as transfer fees, transfer from dividend equalisation, and other reserves, credit for over provision of tax and receipts of capital nature, etc. In order to arrive at a technically better measure of business activity, these need to be excluded from total income, as these are outside the productive activity of the producing unit. However, to keep the comparability of series of profits for U.K. and India, these were included in profits.

Thus, profits defined for this study are inclusive of interest on long term borrowings, provision for taxation, dividends and retained profits and exclude interest on short term borrowings and depreciation.

Capital Employed Defined in this Study

The concept of Capital employed used for this study had to be appropriate to the concept of profits to which it was to be related. Since profits are defined as income accruing on long term investments, the concept of capital required that we include capital of long term nature. Fortunately enough the data for U.K. and India provided required information to derive the long term capital employed. Following concept of capital employed is thus used in this study to derive appropriate rate of profit for U.K. and India.

Capital employed includes total net fixed assets plus net working assets. The net working assets are derived by deducting from current assets the currents liabilities of the industry. This is equivalent to net worth (equity plus reserves and surpluses) plus bonded and long term loans. Since profits are taken net of depreciation and interest on short term borrowings, capital employed also excludes depreciation charges and short term borrowings.

(A) For U.K. Manufacturing Industries

The Capital employed for U.K. manufacturing industries is termed as average net assets and includes net tangible fixed assets goodwill, investment in unconsolidated subsidiaries, stock and work-in-progress, and trade and other debtors, other investment, tax reserve certificates, treasury bills and cash etc. (i.e., current assets) and excludes current liabilities which include bank overdraft, short term loans, trade and other creditors, dividends and interest due and current taxation. These are taken net of depreciation charges. In short, capital employed comprises of net fixed assets plus current assets minus current liabilities.

(B) For Indian Manufacturing Industries

Concept of Capital employed, similar to the one adopted for U.K. is followed for India. It thus includes net fixed assets plus net working assets and excludes depreciation charges.

In other words capital employed for Indian industries comprises of net fixed assets: inventories, loans and advances and other debtor balances, investments, advance of income tax and cash and balance (i.e., current assets) and excludes provision for taxation, other current provisions, short term borrowings, trade dues and other current liabilities (i.e., current liabilities). In other words, capital employed consists of next fixed assets plus current assets minus current liabilities and are taken net of depreciation charges.

Thus series of capital employed, defined in the above manner, were prepared, for each manufacturing industry of U.K. and India for the entire study period so that profits could be related to these for obtaining the long term rate of profit.

(C) Profit Rate Define for this Study

Having prepared the series of profits and capital employed for manufacturing industries of U.K. and India for the period 1960-61 to 1988-89, the next step was to derive a ratio of profits to capital employed and express it in percentage terms. The exercise has carried to all manufacturing industries of both the countries for the study period. The rate of profit thus derive indicates the earning power of capital of long term nature and thus enables us to examine long term profitability better.

3

Towards the Profitability of Indian Manufacturing Industries

1. Introduction

An attempt has been made to examine the trends in rates of profits of nineteen Indian manufacturing industries over the period 1960-61 to 1988-89. Moreover, an attempt has also been made to capture the industrywise variations in the series of profit rates, which reveals the dispersion of the series for each industry over the study period.

Table 3.1 provides data on profit rates of 19 Indian Manufacturing industries for the period 1960-61 to 1988-89, alongwith profitability ratios for five sectors. The last row of Table 3.1 reveals profitability trends in very simple manner. Following conclusions are drawn.

1. Table 3.1 reveals that majority of the industries, 15 out of 19 (i.e., 78.9% industries) industries suffered a percentage point fall in 1988-89 (or 1980-81), while only four industries, viz., Sugar, Tobacco, Other Chemical Products and Rubber and Rubber Products industries enjoyed percentage point rise in the same period.
2. Jute Textiles industry suffered from the biggest decline

Table 3.1 : Rates of Profit for Indian Manufacturing Industries : 1960–61 to 1988–89

(per cent per annum)

Year	Grains & Pulses	Edible Vegetable & Hydrogenated Oils	Sugar	Tobacco	Cotton Textiles	Silk, Rayon and Woollen Textiles	Medicines & Pharmaceutical Preparation	Pottery, China, Earthernware & Structural Clay Products	Paper & Paper Products	Consumer Goods Sector
	1	2	3	4	5	6	7	8	9	
1960–61	31.4	17.8	18.2	18.9	20.3	27.7	29.4	10.8	13.0	19.8
1961–62	20.5	13.3	14.0	17.2	22.0	22.9	28.1	18.4	12.0	19.3
1962–63	16.2	12.7	11.5	21.9	12.8	21.3	26.4	18.7	12.4	14.4
1963–64	21.2	10.6	18.6	16.5	13.8	20.6	32.8	15.3	11.3	15.5
1964–65	36.4	19.6	19.7	23.6	13.8	20.0	35.9	8.8	9.2	16.1
1965–66	22.8	20.1	20.4	27.2	6.0	22.7	44.8	12.0	7.3	14.0
1966–67	24.6	26.6	15.1	21.5	10.4	27.5	43.5	11.1	8.7	16.1
1967–68	13.4	9.0	8.9	26.5	7.3	24.3	37.7	8.8	6.7	13.0
1968–69	11.9	31.8	25.2	27.3	4.8	22.9	39.1	8.3	8.4	14.3
1969–70	9.1	26.3	17.4	24.8	10.6	24.9	45.1	9.3	14.8	17.8
1970–71	16.1	14.7	5.8	26.4	13.6	26.7	36.6	15.2	16.2	17.9
1971–72	17.2	0.1	14.9	26.5	11.2	23.5	33.9	20.1	17.3	17.2
1972–73	4.2	13.4	31.0	15.3	16.2	22.5	32.8	27.0	13.8	19.8

(Contd.)

Table 3.1 : (Contd.)

(per cent per annum)

	1	2	3	4	5	6	7	8	9	
1973–74	6.8	32.2	19.6	22.0	26.1	26.5	30.8	20.3	14.5	21.0
1974–75	9.3	25.0	18.2	17.7	17.9	30.0	28.3	18.9	30.9	22.8
1975–76	–21.6	14.0	6.8	13.8	3.0	13.0	29.8	20.8	24.9	11.7
1976–77	–0.2	22.5	17.6	19.3	2.5	19.2	37.3	23.4	10.6	12.6
1977–78	16.1	24.1	9.3	18.9	11.1	12.8	37.7	26.5	11.9	14.9
1978–79	16.1	18.8	–4.9	23.2	22.6	16.3	39.0	25.5	13.9	19.9
1979–80	9.2	23.1	6.0	22.7	23.9	14.2	35.8	27.4	16.3	21.2
1980–81	7.4	25.0	26.7	21.4	18.7	10.5	26.3	22.6	14.8	18.5
1981–82		18.8	24.8		12.6	7.2	23.9	25.5	9.7	14.9
1982–83		25.9	15.8		6.6	–0.7	26.4	17.8	7.8	10.5
1983–84		12.1	15.4		7.9	8.0	20.1	12.0	4.7	9.5
1984–85		9.5	19.4		5.5	8.5	21.7	9.0	7.0	9.1
1985–86		14.5	26.8		7.8	10.2	21.6	8.5	6.4	10.4
1986–87		11.0	24.5		6.6	7.8	17.7	7.9	4.7	9.1
1987–88		13.7	21.7		4.5	7.9	17.1	7.7	1.7	7.3
1988–89		13.1	20.2		6.3	10.8	19.7	10.0	3.6	7.9
%age point change in 1988–89 over 1960–61	–24.0	–4.7	2.0	2.5	–14.0	–16.9	–9.7	–0.8	–9.4	–11.9

(contd.)

Table 3.1 : (Contd.)

(per cent per annum)

Year	Aluminium	Basic Industrial Chemicals	Cement	BASIC GOODS SECTOR	Transport Equipment	Electrical Machinery Apparatus & Appliances	Machinery other than Transport & Electrical Equipment	Ferrous non-ferrous Metal Products	CAPITAL GOODS SECTOR	Jute Textiles	Other Chemical Products	Rubber & Rubber Products	INTERMEDIARY GOODS SECTOR	WHOLE MANUFACTURING SECTOR
	10	11	12		13	14	15	16		17	18	19		
1960–61	19.7	20.0	11.6	16.0	18.8	21.8	24.3	18.0	20.4	12.4	24.6	16.0	14.6	18.9
1961–62	15.6	18.5	13.1	15.8	20.9	22.2	22.2	17.7	20.8	4.1	22.1	16.6	9.8	18.3
1962–63	16.2	16.1	17.8	16.8	21.7	27.5	24.6	19.1	23.0	32.2	28.3	14.3	27.0	18.0
1963–64	21.4	15.4	16.2	16.5	19.3	33.1	27.6	22.1	23.4	20.9	30.9	15.0	20.5	18.0
1964–65	22.7	17.9	16.2	18.0	21.2	32.5	26.5	24.3	25.3	7.2	25.0	17.6	12.2	18.4
1965–66	16.0	15.8	16.9	16.2	20.1	27.8	17.2	23.2	21.9	7.7	26.2	16.0	15.6	16.8
1966–67	13.6	17.3	21.6	17.4	15.9	22.6	13.7	17.5	17.3	–1.0	24.5	17.9	13.1	16.4
1967–68	14.0	13.5	17.7	14.9	12.6	18.9	9.6	11.4	13.2	–5.5	21.8	23.3	13.2	13.4
1968–69	11.5	11.1	10.5	11.0	10.5	11.8	11.2	9.8	10.8	0.7	21.3	27.1	16.6	12.8
1969–70	14.5	15.8	11.9	14.4	9.1	17.4	14.0	13.2	13.0	–0.5	23.3	25.1	16.7	15.6
1970–71	17.3	16.3	12.8	15.6	13.6	21.6	14.1	21.7	19.9	6.6	22.2	19.6	16.8	17.6

(Contd.)

Table 3.1 : (Contd.)

	10	11	12		13	14	15	16		17	18	19		
1971–72	13.9	17.4	12.8	15.8	14.9	26.1	13.9	23.6	19.1	20.1	26.2	18.7	21.8	17.7
1972–73	12.2	18.4	8.1	15.3	13.4	22.8	16.8	18.3	17.7	3.8	22.2	17.3	15.8	17.7
1973–74	6.0	18.7	2.8	13.7	15.5	21.3	20.8	21.5	19.5	–8.8	24.6	15.7	13.9	18.4
1974–75	2.3	26.1	3.6	18.6	15.8	26.2	23.7	25.2	22.4	18.1	31.5	21.7	25.0	21.9
1975–76	9.3	21.2	2.5	16.8	15.2	22.8	25.6	4.6	18.6	0.7	–11.5	18.2	1.5	14.2
1976–77	19.6	22.7	5.3	19.8	20.7	22.1	29.1	9.8	21.8	–31.6	–11.9	11.1	–5.9	15.9
1977–78	6.6	22.8	18.0	19.8	19.3	23.7	26.1	8.7	20.9	–37.0	29.6	7.8	15.6	18.1
1978–79	15.4	23.2	15.1	21.0	22.9	24.8	25.4	15.3	23.0	–13.5	29.3	16.6	22.1	21.3
1979–80	11.5	20.2	15.1	18.5	22.9	30.4	25.7	20.7	25.4	75.6	29.4	26.7	34.1	22.8
1980–81	3.2	16.5	3.1	13.3	26.3	34.2	26.9	17.9	27.5	24.5	26.3	21.3	24.5	20.5
1981–82		15.2	8.3	14.2	36.5	31.3	29.3	19.0	29.9	–37.9	24.1	25.8	25.4	20.9
1982–83		12.4	23.4	14.7	23.7	22.9	21.4	9.7	20.8	–73.8	19.5	42.9	19.5	15.8
1983–84		10.4	16.4	11.9	17.8	16.5	17.4	5.2	15.8	–13.6	25.6	11.1	14.7	12.7
1984–85		13.8	9.8	12.7	17.7	14.8	13.8	8.8	14.7	–10.7	23.2	5.8	11.5	12.1
1985–86		13.0	9.1	12.0	14.9	12.9	10.3	11.4	12.5	–32.8	27.4	10.5	13.4	11.7
1986–87		8.5	5.5	7.8	14.0	12.4	9.3	12.8	11.9	–20.3	26.7	14.4	16.1	10.1
1987–88		8.2	3.7	7.1	12.5	14.1	10.9	12.5	12.3	–37.6	25.8	14.5	15.7	9.4

(Contd.)

Table 3.1 : (Contd.)

	10	11	12		13	14	15	16		17	18	19		
1988–89		11.9	0.4	9.1	14.6	13.7	12.2	15.0	13.7	–14.8	29.7	20.2	21.8	11.1
%age point change in 1988–89 over 1960–61	–16.5	–8.1	–11.2	–6.9	–4.2	–8.1	–12.1	–3.0	–6.7	–27.2	5.1	4.2	7.2	–7.8

Sources:

1. Financial Statistics of Joint Stock Companies in India covering the period 1960-61 to 1970-71, 1970-71 to 1974-75 in two volume published by R.B.I. in 1975 and 1977.
2. Various issues of R.B.I. Bulletin for the period 1975-76 to 1980-81, viz., May 1980, November 1981 and July 1983.
3. Computer print out sent by Company Finance Department of R.B.I. for period 1981-82 to 1988-89.

Notes:

1. The data on Grains and Pulses, Tobacco and Aluminium are available upto 1980-81 only, i.e., for Twenty one years only while for the remaining sixteen industries data are available upto 1988-89, i.e., for twenty nine years.
2. Profit rates for various sectors are weighted rates and are worked out as ratios of summation of Profits of industries in each sector to summation of capital employed in industries of respective sectors. Please see the text for details.
3. Profit rates are rounded up for one digit after decimal point.
4. Only medium and large public limited companies with paidup capital of Rs. 0.5 million or above are covered.

in Profit rate of 27.2 percentage point while Pottery, China, Earthen-ware and Structure Clay Products industry had lowest fall of 0.8 percentage points in 1988-89 over 1960-61.

3. Other Chemical Products had the largest rise of 5.1 percentage points in profitability in 1988-89 over 1960-61 while Sugar industry had the lowest rise of 2.0 percentage points in the same period.

4. Amongst the sectors, all the four sectors except Intermediary Goods sector had a fall in profit rate in 1988-89 over 1960-61, with Consumers Goods Sector suffering the largest fall of 11.9 percentage points, while basic and Capital goods sector experienced lowest and almost equal decline of 6.9 and 6.7 percentage points respectively while Whole manufacturing sector suffered from a fall of 7.8 per centage points over the same period.

5. Intermediary Goods Sector alone enjoyed a rise in profit rate in 1988-89 to the tune of 7.2 percentage points over 1960-61, due to rise in profitability of 2 out of 3 industries in 1988-89 over 1960-61, of which it comprises.

6. Ten industries had a fall in profitability which stood above the fall experienced by Whole Manufacturing Sector in 1988-89 over 1960-61, while six industries had below it.

While summing up the results of Table 3.1 it can be said that majority of the manufacturing industries and sectors in India experienced worsening of their long term earning power in 1988-89 as compared to 1960-61. However, these findings relate only to two different years, i.e., the end and beginning year of the study period, and hence, do not reflect trends in profitability over the whole period under study. This has tempted us to undertake Time Trend Regression Analysis of Profitability. Similar exercises are later on carried out for U.K. manufacturing industries which would facilitate comparative analysis.

It is however felt that a brief discussion about the classical hypothesis regarding tendency of profit rate for various industries over a long period will be appropriate before we take up the trend analysis further. These are discussed briefly in the following section.

Tendency of Profit Rates to Fall in the Long Run : A Classical Hypothesis

Right from Adam Smith, most of the classical economists have argued that under a competitive market system, craze for capital accumulation, and, competition among the producers, causes the rate of profit to fall to a very low level, almost to zero, in the long run. According to Adam Smith, as the society progresses, the production expands and this leads to an increase in demand for labourers. Consequently, the wages rise, stimulating the population growth and causing expansion of markets. This leads to the off shoot of division of labour and large scale production, and sets in cumulative growth process. Since the production process requires longer time, capitalists are required to stock capital and provide it to productive labourers who add to the output. Thus, capital accumulation sets into the process. The economy operates under the conditions of perfect competition with invisible hand, i.e., price-profit mechanism, in full operation. Producers compete for investing into higher profitable industries, causing the levelling down of rates of profit in various branches of production. Wages are lowered due to increase in labour supply via increased population. The process of growth through perfect competition, thus continues till profit rates are brought down to a minimum, and wages to the subsistence level. According to Adam Smith, profitability tends to fall overtime as the society advance.

Similar tendency of rates of profit to fall over a long period of time was assumed by another great classical economist viz., David Ricardo. According to him, as the society progresses, population expands fast as the wages are above the subsistence level. However, due to the application of law of diminishing returns to agriculture, food production increases slowly. Capitalists accumulate capital for supporting the labourers, or, for giving advances to them during the production process, and, earn a sufficient rate of profit on their capital. The society operates under competitive forces. In the beginning, high profits attract more capital and thus cause more capital accumulation. Consequently, demand for labourers increases and wages are pushed up above the subsistence level. The result is, rise in population, increase in demand for food, resort to lower and inferior quality land (with the law of diminishing returns in operation), and, rise in rents on land. The whole produce is divided between wages and profits after rents are paid. As the rents rise, the amount left for profits and wages is reduced. On the other hand, expansion of population results in pushing down of wages to subsistence level. Rents turnout to be very high while profits fall to a very low level, hence, no incentive is left to producers for further capital accumulation. The society thus reaches "Stationery State", with very high rents, subsistence wages and very low or zero rates of profit. Hence, Ricardo assumed that rate of profit for an industry has a tendency to fall over a long period of time.

Karl Marx, the founder of communist ideology, and, a well-known critic of classical writers also assumed that profitability of an industry would fall over a long period of time. According to him, the growth process occurs through class struggle. He believed in labour theory of value. According to Marx, labour alone is the source of value and is paid in wages its own value, socially necessary for rearing, training and maintaining its life. The capitalists exploit the labourers they employ and extract surplus value in the form of profits. Their main aim is to extract maximum surplus value from the labourers. This is achieved through accumulation of capital in two basic forms of capital, viz., variable capital (V) in the form of labour and constant capital, C, (i.e. Raw materials, tools, machines, etc.). As a result, production increases greatly due to use of machines, causing technological unemployment in the form of industrial reserve army. In this process, constant capital (C) which produces only its own value replaces labour which is the only source of surplus value. Obviously, constant capital acts as two edged sword for the capitalist, as on one side, it causes unemployment, low wages and continuous exploitation of labour, while on the other side it fails to fulfil capitalists ultimate purpose, i.e., creation of surplus value. According to Marx, there is a long run tendency under capitalism to employ constant capital in relatively increased amounts than variable capital. This results in continuous expansion of organic composition of capital i.e., the ratio

$$\frac{\text{Constant Capital}}{\text{Constant Capital } + \text{ Variable Capital}} \text{ or } \left(\frac{C}{C+V}\right), \text{ i.e., the}$$

proportion of constant capital in total capital. Consequently, the amount of surplus value created falls, causing a fall in rate of profit over time. Marx defined rate of profit as a ratio of surplus value(s) to total capital (C+V), i.e., $\frac{S}{C+V}$, and argued that it falls over time. It other words, capitalists passion for capital accumulation for extracting more and more surplus value, itself results into fall in the rate of profit overtime.

Alfred Marshall also expressed the views similar to classical economists. According to him, in the long run, the principle of factor substitution, compels the rates of profit to move towards a central value. Assuming that supply of entrepreneurs is highly elastic in the long run, he explains, how, competitive forces and factor substitution results in wiping out of abnormal profits and results in levelling of rates of profit among different industries towards the Central value.

The above discussed thoughts of classical and neoclassical economists provide a hypothesis that under competitive conditions, rates of profits of industries have a tendency to fall over long run. The present study, however, does not intend to test the validity of this hypothesis, because, the assumptions underlying this hypothesis, viz., presence of perfect competition, does not hold true for any of the countries of the world, today, while duration of long run is not well defined and specified. Moreover, these economists assumed the existence of industries with similar age structure, while the case is different for India as well as for U.K. and between India and U.K. The industries examined in this study have great variations in their inception periods and age structure. As regards India, industrialisation has been a recent phenomenon, the outcome of development planning undertaken since 1950's. On the other hand, U.K. had been world leader in the process of industrialisation since 18th century. Moreover, business entities, as well as the surrounding economic conditions in both the countries have been entirely different from what the classical economists visualised in their times. Finally, the concept of profit rate envisaged by classical writers related to the real concept while this study relies on the financial concept of profit rate wherein variations are not eliminated.

Considering the experience of more than 215 years of industrilization by U.K., one may expect that long term profit rates considered for this study may reveal falling tendency for U.K.

As regards India, the author's earlier study (Rede, 79, 1984) which covered a period of 1950-51 to 1977-78, revealed that majority of basic and capital goods industries (12 out of 20 industries examined) had a rising trend in profit rate. However the concept of profit rate and the time period covered were both different from the ones used in this study.[1] These changes are expected to give results different from the earlier study. This is so, because, earlier study covered the period when the Indian industries were in the stage of infancy, while this study covers the period after this stage is passed and industries have reached the stage of adulthood.

Finally, the differences in the economic conditions of India and U.K. in terms of competition, direct government intervention, regulation and support to industries, existence of entrepreneurial skills, institutional setups, technical, managerial, organisational, professional and marketing skills, etc., are likely to get reflected via their influence on the profit rates. This has tempted us to examine and compare the trends in profitability of manufacturing industries of these two countries. However, it is felt that the results based on the empirical data and surrounding economic conditions of entirely different type than assumed by the classical authors should not be used either to refute, or to accept their hypthesis. However, given the data for India and U.K., we can examine the behaviour of

1. The earlier study used gross profit rate and covered the period 1950-51 to 1977-78 while this study relies on long term profit rate and covers the period 1960-61 to 1988-89.

the earning rates of manufacturing industries of two countries with different economic ideologies, stage of economic development and industrialisation, technology, etc. This, we are sure, would lead to very interesting conclusions.

Estimates of Trend Coefficients for Indian Manufacturing Industries

An attempt has been made in this section to estimate the trend coefficients of rates of profit in Indian Manufacturing Industries by fitting a linear regression model. The Linear Model fitted is as follows:

$$P = \alpha + \beta t + e$$

Where P is rate of profit, t is the time, and α and β are the parameters (intercept and coefficients respectively) and e is the error term. The results of the application of above stated model to the profitability of Indian manufacturing industries are presented in Table 3.2. Following conclusions are derived.

1. Table 3.2 reveals that the Linear Model of Time Trend of Profitability has proved to be a "good fit" in case of eight out of nineteen industries, i.e., 42.1% of the industries examined here. This is revealed from the value of R^2, the coefficient of determination.

2. All these eight industries, viz., Grains and Pulses, Silk Rayon and Woollen Textiles, Medicines and Pharmaceutical Preparation (Consumers, goods industries), Aluminium, Cement (Basic Goods Industries), Electrical Machinery, Apparatus and Appliances, Ferrous/Non-Ferrous Metal Products (Capital Goods Industries), and Jute Textile (Intermediary Goods Sector), experienced a strong tendency in profitability to decline over the study period. The negative values of β, the time trend coefficient, confirms this as these are observed to be statistically significant.

Statistically significant negative values of β, the time trend coefficient thus indicate strong negative relationship between profitability and time over the study period.

Table 3.2 : Results of Regression of Rates of Profit on Time for Indian Manufacturing Industries : 1960–61 to 1988–89

Ind. Sr. No.	Industry	$P = \alpha + \beta t + e$			
		α	β	R^2	F-Value
1	2	3	4	5	6
1.	Grains and Pulses	26.691** (6.096)	–1.179** (–3.382)	0.376**	11.441**
2.	Edible Vegetable and Hydrogenated oils	18.767** (6.507)	–0.057 (–0.341)	0.004	0.116
3.	Sugar	14.661** (4.992)	0.145 (0.855)	0.026	0.727
4.	Tobacco	22.153** (11.714)	–0.055 (–0.363)	0.006	0.131
5.	Cotton Textiles	15.551** (6.326)	–0.240 (–1.679)	0.094	2.821
6.	Silk, Rayon & Woollen Textiles	28.824** (15.277)	–0.749** (–6.826)	0.633**	46.60**
7.	Medicines & Pharmaceutical Preparations	39.865** (16.263)	–0.590** (–4.136)	0.387**	17.109**
8.	Pottery, China, Earthenware & Structural Clay Products	15.771** (5.986)	0.023 (0.153)	0.0008	0.023
9.	Paper & Paper Products	14.629** (6.396)	–0.206 (–1.549)	0.081	2.401
	CONSUMER GOODS SECTOR	19.228** (13.512)	–0.278** (–3.359)	0.294**	11.288**
10.	Aluminium	19.629** (9.700)	–0.561** (–3.484)	0.389**	12.141**
11.	Basic Industrial Chemicals	19.245** (11.966)	–0.183 (–1.959)	0.124	3.840
12.	Cement	16.041** (7.394)	–0.312* (–2.473)	0.184*	6.116*
	BASIC GOODS SECTOR	17.985** (15.547)	–0.199** (–2.965)	0.245**	8.791**
13.	Transport Equipment	17.317** (8.139)	0.046 (0.372)	0.005	0.138

(Contd.)

Table 3.2 : (Contd.)

Ind. Sr. No.	Industry	$P = \alpha + \beta t + e$			
		α	β	R^2	F-Value
1	2	3	4	5	6
14.	Electrical Machinery, Apparatus & Appliances	26.902** (11.663)	–0.298* (–2.224)	0.154*	4.949*
15.	Machinery (Other than Transport and Electrical Equipment)	22.035** (8.720)	–0.173 (–1.178)	0.048	1.389
16.	Ferrous/Non-Ferrous Metal Products	20.574** (10.191)	–0.318* (–2.710)	0.213*	7.345*
	CAPITAL GOODS SECTOR	21.303** (1.315)	--0.141 (1.285)	0.057	1.652
17.	Jute Textiles	19.385 (2.047)	–1.532** (–2.781)	0.222**	7.735*
18.	Other Chemical Products	22.962** (5.862)	0.004 (0.020)	0.000	0.0004
19.	Rubber & Rubber Products	18.551** (6.714)	–0.021 (–0.131)	0.0006	0.017
	INTERMEDIARY GOODS SECTOR	15.375** (5.244)	0.084 (0.494)	0.008	0.244
	WHOLE MANUFACTURING SECTOR	18.992** (15.136)	–0.172* (–2.365)	0.171*	5.595*

Source : Table 3.1

Notes : 1. Figures in Brackets are t values.

2. ** Indicates that estimate is significant at 1% level.

3. * Indicates at estimate is significant at 5% level.

4. Industries like Grains & Pulses, Tobacco and Aluminium cover the period 1960–61 to 1980–81 while others cover the period 1960–61 to 1988–89.

Table 3.2 further reveals that β assumes different values (negative) for different industries and ranges in values from 0.298 for Electrical Machinery, Apparatus and Appliances, to –1.179 for Grains and Pulses industry (covering the period 1960-61 to 1980-81) during the study period. This implies that profitability of different industries declined at different rates over this period.

4. Only in case of 4 industries, viz., Sugar, Pottery, China, Earthernware and Structural Clay Products, Transport Equipment and Other Chemical Products, the sign for β, the time trend coefficient is positive, implying a tendency of profit rate to rise over time. However, β being statistically non-significant, the result are not discussed. In case of eleven industries, no definite trend could be observed as the results are statistically non significant.

5. The value of coefficient of determination, R^2, varied in case of industries having strong declining tendency of profit rate over time, from 0.154 for Electrical machinery, Apparatus and Appliances to 0.633 for Silk-Rayon and Woollen Textiles industry. Such great variation in the value of R^2 implies that time explains profitability variations of different industries in different degree over the time. This means that time explains variations in profitability of the above two industries to the extent of 15.4% and 63.3 respectively over the study period.

6. Sectorwise time trend regression results are also presented in Table 3.2. It may be noted from this table that out of Five Sectors shown, the Consumer and basic Goods Sectors, as well as the Whole Manufacturing Sector, all had a strong tendency for profit rate to fall over the study period as the results for R^2, the coefficient of determination and β, are statistically significant, while results are non significant for other two sectors.

7. The value of R^2 varies between 0.171 (Whole Manufacturing Sector) to 0.294 (Consumer Goods Sector), indicating that time explains profitability variations of these sectors to the tune of 17.1% and 29.4% respectively.

8. β the time trend coefficient also varies in value from −0.172 (Whole Manufacturing Sector) to −0.278 (Consumers Goods Sector, indicating that as time increases, profit rates of sectors fall between this range.

Dispersions in Rates of Profits of Indian Manufacturing Industries

This section of the chapter intends to examine the industrywise dispersions in rates of profit of Indian Manufacturing industries over the study period of 29 years. This is achieved through estimation of mean, standard deviation and coefficient of variation. The estimates are presented in Table 3.3.

Table 3.3 : Industrywise Variation in Profitability of Indian Manufacturing Sector : 1960–61 to 1988–89

Ind. S.No.	*Industry*	*Mean*	*S.D.*	*C.V.*
1.	Grains & Pulses	13.7	11.6	0.849
2.	Edible Vegetable & Hydrogenated Oils	17.9	7.3	0.409
3.	Sugar	16.8	7.5	0.447
4.	Tobacco	21.6	4.0	0.185
5.	Cotton Textiles	11.9	6.5	0.547
6.	Silk, Rayon & Woollen Textiles	17.6	7.9	0.449
7.	Medicines & Pharmaceutical Preparations	31.0	7.9	0.256
8.	Pottery, China, Earthenware & Structural Clay Products	16.1	6.7	0.414
9.	Paper & Paper Products	11.5	6.0	0.524
	CONSUMER GOODS SECTOR	15.1	4.3	0.285
10.	Aluminium	13.5	5.4	0.405
11.	Basic Industrial Chemicals	16.5	4.4	0.264
12.	Cement	11.4	6.1	0.536
	BASIC GOODS SECTOR	15.0	3.4	0.225
13.	Transport Equipment	18.0	5.4	0.300
14.	Electrical Machinery, Apparatus and Appliances	22.4	6.4	0.283
15.	Machinery (Other than transport and Electrical Equipment)	19.4	6.6	0.337
16.	Ferrous/Non-Ferrous Metal Products	15.8	5.8	0.365
	CAPITAL GOODS SECTOR	19.2	4.9	0.256
17.	Jute Textiles	–3.6	27.2	–7.548

(Contd.)

Table 3.3 : (Contd.)

Ind. S.No.	*Industry*	*Mean*	*S.D.*	*C.V.*
18.	Other Chemical Products	23.0	9.9	0.430
19.	Rubber & Rubber Products	18.2	7.0	0.384
	INTERMEDIARY GOODS SECTOR	16.6	7.5	0.448
	WHOLE MANUFACTURING SECTOR	16.4	3.5	0.215

Source : Table 3.1

Notes : 1. Mean = $\overline{P} = \dfrac{\sum_{j=1}^{n} P_j}{n}$ where P_j = Rate of Profits for j^{th} industry.

n = Number of years.

2. S.D. = Standard Deviation = $\sigma = \sqrt{\dfrac{\Sigma(P_j - \overline{P})^2}{n}}$

3. C.V. = Coefficient of Variation = $\overline{P}/\sigma$

The mean rates of profit are derived by summing up the profit rates of each industry over time and then dividing this by the number of years, i.e., 29 or 21 years as the case may be. This indicates average profitability of the industry over the period. Following results are derived from Table 3.3.

1. It is observed from Table 3.3 that, on an average, medicine and Pharmaceutical Preparations Industry experienced highest profit rate (31%), while Jute Textiles Industry suffered from the lowest and negative rate of profit (-3.6%) over the study period.
2. The Whole Manufacturing Sector, on an average, enjoyed 16.% rate of profit. Amongst, the sector, Capital Goods Sector (19.2%) and Intermediary Goods Sector (16.6%), on an average, had profit rate above the Whole Manufacturing Sector, while Consumer Goods Sector (15.1%) and Basic Goods Sector (15.0%) had below it.
3. Out of total 19 industries examined, 11 industries, i.e., (57.9% industries) viz., Edible Vegetable and hydrogenat-

ed Oils, Sugar, Tobacco, Silk-Rayon and Woollen Textiles, Medicines, and Pharmaceutical Preparation (Consumers Goods Sector), Basic Industrial Chemicals (Basic Goods Sectors), Transport Equipment, Electrical Machinery, Apparatus and Appliances, Machinery (Other than Transport and Electrical Equipment) Capital Goods Sector), Other Chemical Products and Rubber & Rubber Products (Intermediary Goods Sector), enjoyed, on an average, a higher rate of profit than Whole Manufacturing Sector.

It may further be noted here that, on an average, majority of Capital Goods Sector (3 out of 4 i.e., 75%) and one Basic Goods Sector industries experienced higher profit rate than Whole Manufacturing Sector, while only 5 out of 9 Consumer Goods Industries, i.e., 55.6%, experienced the same.

4. Another important observation which follows from Table 3.3 is that mean rates of Profit vary greatly in case of all the industries under examination, irrespective of the sector of which these belong.

Once the examination of average earnings positions of different Indian manufacturing industries is completed, it becomes essential to study the year to year variations in these earnings rates over the whole period. Standard Deviation and Coefficient of Variation, are the two measures of dispersions, which enable us to achieve this. The former measures absolute dispersion while the latter provides relative dispersion in the series. Hence, the estimates of standard deviation and coefficient of Variation for profit rate series of each Indian manufacturing industry over the study period are worked out and presented in Table 3.3. These measures reveal the extent of variation of actual values of profit rates of each industry from its mean value of the series. Since Coefficient of Variation (C.V.) is more useful in comparative analysis, we discuss below its significance for Indian industries. The higher values of coefficient of variation indicate larger dispersion among the profit rate series of respective industries and vice-versa.

Following observations are made from Table 3.3.

1. Tobacco, with coefficient of variation being 0.185 experienced lowest variations in profit rates over the study period while Jute Textiles Industry, with lowest and negative mean Profit rate, suffered from largest dispersions, coefficient of variation assuming value equal to -7.58.

2. Amongst the sectors, the Whole Manufacturing sector had lowest variations in profit rates (Coefficient of Variations = 0.215) while Intermediary Goods Sector suffered from largest variations (coefficient of Variation -0.48) during the study period.

3. If we arbitrarily divide these 19 industries into Relatively stable (C.V. with value upto 0.250), Moderately fluctuating (C.V. lying between 0.251 and 0.500), Highly fluctuating (C.V. lying between 0.501 and 0.750) and Erratically fluctuating (C.V. above 0.750), then it is observed from Table 3.3 that, Tabacco alone experienced relatively stable variations in profit rates. Majority of the industries, 13 out of 19 industries (68.4%) experienced moderately fluctuating variations in profit rate series. These industries are Edible Vegetable and Hydrogenated Oils, Sugar, Silk-Rayon and Woollen Textiles, Medicines and Pharmaceutical Preparations, Pottery, Chine, Earthenware and Structural Clay Products (5 out of 9 Consumers Goods Sectors Industries), Aluminium, Basic Industrial Chemicals, (2 out of 3 Industries belonging to Basic Goods Sector), Transport Equipment, Electrical Machinery, Apparatus and Appliances, Machinery (Other than Transport and Electrical Equipment) Ferrous/Non-Ferrous Metal Products (All, i.e., 4 industries belonging to Capital Goods Sector), Other Chemical Products and Rubber and Rubber Products (2 out of 3 industries belonging to Intermediary Goods Sector).

Three industries, viz., Cotton Textiles, Paper and Paper Products (Consumer Goods Sector) and Cement (Basic Goods Sector) and highly fluctuating series of Profit rate, while Jute

Textiles (Intermediary Goods Sector) alone reveals the most erratically fluctuating series.

As far as the sector variations are concerned, Whole Manufacturing Sector exhibits lowest dispersion (C.V. =0.215) and Intermediary Goods Sector had highest variations (C.V.=0.448). Basic Goods Sections and Whole Manufacturing Sector revealed relatively stable profitability series while the other three sectors, viz., consumer, capital and intermediary goods sector, experienced moderately fluctuating series of profit rates over the study period.

In sum, the profitability trends in Indian manufacturing sector reveal that most of these industries have a tendency for rates of profit to fall over a long period, as in case of all the cases (8 industries for which regression results are statistically significant, reveal strong declining trend of profitability over the study period). Moreover, time explains this fall in profitability at various degrees. Finally, most of the industries, 68.4%, experienced moderate fluctuations in profitability series while only 3 industries had highly fluctuating series.

4

Towards the Profitability of U.K. Manufacturing Industries

I. Introduction

This chapter is devoted to the examination of trends and variations in the profit of U.K. manufacturing industries. It is a well-known fact that U.K. was the initiator of industrialisation in the world some 215 years ago, and the same country has taken the pride in fuelling the engine of privatisation in early 1980's. With capitalist form of its economy, U.K.'s manufacturing sector has been working under highly competitive market conditions, though these are not as perfect as envisaged by the classical authors. Obviously, price-profit mechanism is at the center of all manufacturing activities. The country is advanced in technology, economic development and industrialization and enjoys relatively high levels of national and per capita income. Being the ruler of a number of colonies till half of this century, England commanded lot of markets for its manufactured products which could be produced cheaply via imports of cheap raw materials, from the colonies she ruled. Consequently, high profit rates could be reaped overtime. However, the country lost control over most of her colonies by 1950's and has been facing keen competition in world market from other industrialized European countries, U.S.A. etc. since early twentieth century. Japan turned out to be one of the biggest competitor of these countries after World War II. In sum, though U.K. is enjoying better economic conditions than India, she has suffered a set back to her industrialization after Second World War.

Keeping in mind the back-ground stated above, we take up the examination of profitability trends of U.K. manufacturing industries. Table 4.1 provides data on profit rates of 17 U.K. manufacturing industries for the period 1960-61 to 1988-89, i.e., 29 years, alongwith profitability ratios for five sectors. The last row of this table indicates the profitability trends in very simple way. Following observations are made:

1. It is observed from Table 4.1 that 10 out of 17 industries (i.e., 58.8%) industries) enjoyed a percentage point rise in 1988-89, while seven industries (41.2%) suffered percentage point decline in profitability over these years.

   Industries like Food, Timber Furniture, Tobacco, Textiles, Leather, Leather Goods and Fur, Paper Printing and Publishing (Consumer Goods Sector), Metal Manufacture, Chemical and Allied Industries (Basic Goods Sector), Electrical Engineering including Electronics (Capital Goods Sector) and other Manufacturing industries (Intermediary Goods Sector), enjoyed increase in profitability while majority of the capital goods industries (4 out of 5), and 3 consumer goods industries suffered a set back to their earning power of 1988-89 over 1960-61.

   Tobacco enjoyed the largest rise (11.4 percentage points) in profit rate in 1988-89 over 1960-61 while Leather, Leather Goods and Fur industry had smallest rise of 0.5 percentage points during the same period.

3. Ship Building and Marine Engineering suffered a largest decline of 15.2 percentage points in 1988-89 over 1960-61 while Non-Electrical Engineering had the smallest fall of 0.5 percentage points in this period. (Bricks, Pottery, Glass, Ceramics industry had fall in profitability by 0.1 percentage point in 1976-77 over 1960-61).

Table 4.1 : Rates of Profit for U.K. Manufacturing Industries : 1960–61 to 1988–89

(per cent per annum)

Year	INDUSTRIES												
	Food	Drink	Timber Furniture	Tobacco	Textiles	Clothing & Footwear	Leather, Leather GOODS & Fur	Bricks, Pottery, Glass, Ceramics	Paper Printing & Publishing	CONSUMER GOODS SECTOR	Metal Manufacture	Chemical & Allied Industries	BASIC GOODS SECTOR
	1	2	3	4	5	6	7	8	9		10	11	
1960–61	16.4	15.6	16.1	15.3	13.3	20.6	10.0	18.3	15.4	13.3	16.3	15.3	15.7
1961–62	15.6	14.4	12.7	16.5	12.1	18.2	9.7	17.9	14.0	14.6	12.7	12.0	12.3
1962–63	15.7	13.7	10.2	15.8	10.7	13.7	8.0	15.7	12.7	13.5	8.9	11.3	10.3
1963–64	15.8	13.9	12.3	16.1	12.7	12.9	14.3	16.0	12.6	14.0	8.5	12.3	10.8
1964–65	14.6	15.0	16.0	17.0	14.3	15.2	17.0	18.0	14.0	15.1	10.7	13.5	12.4
1965–66	14.6	14.0	14.2	16.8	14.1	13.0	14.7	16.4	13.4	14.4	10.6	12.6	12.4
1966–67	12.6	12.3	11.5	16.6	12.1	10.9	12.2	14.1	11.8	12.4	7.7	10.7	9.66
1967–68	13.1	12.0	12.1	12.3	12.0	12.2	9.6	14.5	11.0	12.3	10.7	11.1	11.0
1968–69	14.1	12.9	15.6	12.5	15.6	13.6	16.7	15.0	12.3	13.7	11.8	13.9	13.5
1969–70	12.9	12.8	12.9	14.4	14.1	13.3	19.7	13.1	11.4	13.0	13.0	13.8	13.6
1970–71	11.9	13.4	12.6	14.0	11.5	12.6	17.2	13.6	10.1	12.3	11.4	11.6	11.6

(Contd.)

Table 4.1 : (Contd.)

(per cent per annum)

1	2	3	4	5	6	7	8	9		10	11		
1971–72	12.6	14.7	20.9	15.4	13.0	16.1	22.3	17.0	10.0	13.6	10.6	11.6	11.4
1972–73	16.0	17.1	36.8	16.9	16.4	13.7	27.9	19.1	13.9	16.3	11.5	12.9	12.6
1973–74	16.0	16.7	35.5	19.6	21.2	15.4	26.2	19.3	17.0	18.0	17.1	17.9	17.7
1974–75	16.0	13.5	21.8	11.2	17.8	11.3	20.2	12.7	16.5	14.8	14.3	23.4	21.6
1975–76	18.5	14.5	18.8	14.7	9.1	10.0	22.8	14.8	11.7	14.3	11.3	17.1	16.0
1976–77	22.5	16.6	23.1	15.8	15.0	10.0	27.8	18.2	15.8	18.0	14.3	19.3	18.4
1977–78	16.9	17.5	16.6	18.9	13.5	9.5	25.0		19.7	17.4	15.5	19.3	18.5
1978–79	18.0	18.0	18.9	18.5	13.7	21.8	17.9		23.1	18.4	13.0	16.9	16.1
1979–80	17.3	16.7	19.9	20.9	11.8	16.9	23.3		17.2	17.6	11.5	15.5	14.8
1980–81	14.8	12.2	7.6	16.9	3.0	13.6	5.0		8.7	11.4	2.9	6.9	6.2
1981–82	17.9	12.3	7.9	21.0	7.8	17.7	10.2		13.1	15.6	–0.8	13.3	11.0
1982–83	16.9	12.3	10.1	23.8	8.2	10.6	2.2		13.6	15.9	–2.2	12.7	11.2
1983–84	15.8	13.7	15.5	22.1	13.3	12.9	12.8		19.2	16.7	5.4	16.0	15.1
1984–85	18.4	14.2	15.1	25.0	18.1	8.6	17.6		18.7	18.5	11.6	19.3	18.6
1985–86	19.2	14.5	14.7	16.4	16.6	16.0	20.4		18.8	16.9	12.7	19.0	18.3
1986–87	19.0	13.3	17.8	22.2	16.3	16.2	19.6		21.8	18.1	7.8	19.7	18.5
1987–88	18.9	17.4	18.5	22.2	21.2	16.3	14.8		22.5	19.6	18.3	23.7	23.1
1988–89	20.2	12.9	18.9	26.7	15.0	16.1	10.5		20.2	20.3	17.4	24.9	23.8
%age Point change in 1988–89 over 1960–61	3.8	–2.7	2.8	11.4	1.7	–4.5	0.5	–0.1	4.8	7.0	1.1	9.6	8.1

Table 4.1 : (Contd.)

Year	INDUSTRIES							
	Vehicles	Electrical Engineering including Electronics	Non-Electrical Engineering	Metal Goods Not Elsewhere specified	Ship Building and Marine Engineering	CAPITAL GOODS SECTOR	Other Manufacturing Industries (I.G.S.)	WHOLE MANUFACTURING SECTOR
	12	13	14	15	16		17	
1960–61	19.2	13.0	15.6	19.9	10.9	16.1	13.8	14.8
1961–62	11.5	11.4	14.6	16.3	9.0	13.0	12.7	13.4
1962–63	9.6	12.4	12.3	15.1	5.4	11.8	11.8	12.1
1963–64	14.7	13.4	12.2	15.2	5.1	13.2	13.2	12.9
1964–65	16.1	15.2	12.3	17.9	3.3	14.4	15.3	14.2
1965–66	15.3	13.7	13.1	16.4	–4.3	13.5	13.5	13.4
1966–67	12.0	13.3	12.3	14.8	0.8	12.5	12.2	11.7
1967–68	8.9	13.4	11.8	14.8	5.3	11.9	12.4	11.9
1968–69	13.1	15.8	12.2	15.3	7.9	13.8	14.7	13.7
1969–70	12.7	13.7	14.2	16.5	–11.0	13.6	13.8	13.3
1970–71	3.0	13.7	12.8	17.0	–0.7	12.1	13.5	12.1
1971–72	10.4	14.0	13.0	16.6	–6.4	13.3	13.5	13.1
1972–73	10.8	18.0	14.7	16.8	14.0	15.8	14.2	15.3
1973–74	13.4	19.4	16.9	18.9	–13.5	17.2	14.8	17.6

(Contd.)

Table 4.1 : (Contd.)

	12	13	14	15	16		17	
1974–75	4.5	17.6	17.1	21.9	20.2	16.5	14.2	16.7
1975–76	–4.6	17.8	16.3	16.1	–2.5	14.2	14.6	14.6
1976–77	5.0	22.7	19.4	17.2	6.5	19.7	18.8	18.6
1977–78	22.8	22.3	23.4	13.3	11.2	21.3	18.5	19.0
1978–79	16.7	20.1	18.8	13.2	2.3	17.0	13.1	17.3
1979–80	10.6	20.2	16.5	14.3	0.1	16.5	13.4	16.5
1980–81	–10.7	17.6	12.5	10.5	–2.9	9.8	10.3	10.2
1981–82	–6.2	18.9	12.7	7.8	–5.8	–2.2	10.6	8.3
1982–83	–2.2	20.5	7.6	6.5	–30.4	9.7	5.7	12.4
1983–84	1.9	22.3	9.5	6.8	–5.3	12.4	10.9	14.7
1984–85	8.1	23.7	12.3	9.4	–5.6	16.4	16.7	17.8
1985–86	9.6	21.2	14.5	11.1	–5.6	15.7	26.0	17.1
1986–87	–0.5	18.8	11.3	13.3	–5.9	11.5	18.3	15.9
1987–88	9.9	21.3	13.8	17.6	–5.6	16.2	21.2	19.2
1988–89	16.8	22.3	15.1	19.2	–4.3	18.6	21.8	20.6
%age Point Change in 1988–89 over 1960–61	–2.4	9.3	–0.5	–0.7	–15.2	2.5	8.0	5.7

Source: Business Monitor, Company Finance, Various issues published by H.M.S.O., London, U.K.

Notes: 1. The data on Bricks, Pottery, Glass and Ceramics were available for the period 1960-61 to 1976-77, while for all other industries for the period 1960-61 to 1988-89.
2. Sectoral division of industries is based on the one followed for Indian Manufacturing Industries.
3. Sectoral Rates of Profits are weighted rates as is the case for Indian Industries.
4. Profit rates are rounded up for one digit after decimal.
5. Intermediary goods sector includes only one industry viz., Other Manufacturing industries, i.e., industry No. 17.

4. All the five sectors enjoyed an increase in profitability in 1988-89 over 1960-61, with Basic Goods Sector having biggest rise of 8.1 percentage points and Capital Good Sector having the lowest increase of 2.5 percentage points in 1988-89 over 1960-61.

5. Only four industries had a rise in profitability above that enjoyed by Whole Manufacturing Sector while six industries had below it.

In short, majority of U.K. manufacturing industries and all the sectors enjoyed improvement in the earning power of long term capital in 1988-89 over 1960-61. In order to capture year to year variations in profit rates of U.K. manufacturing industries an analysis of Time Trend of Profitability is undertaken by fitting a simple linear bivariate regression mode to profitability ratios of each U.K. manufacturing industry over the study period. The results are briefed in Table 4.2.

Table 4.2 : Results of Regression of Rates of Profit on Time for U.K. Manufacturing Industries : 1960–61 to 1988–89

Ind. Sr. No.	Industry	$P = \alpha + \beta t + e$			
		α	β	R^2	F–Value
1	2	3	4	5	6
1.	Food	13.566** (17.738)	0.181** (4.083)	0.381**	16.678
2.	Drink	14.171** (20.251)	0.016 (0.402)	0.006	0.162
3.	Timber Furniture	15.605** (6.048)	0.073 (0.490)	0.009	0.241
4.	Tobacco	13.064** (12.242)	0.316** (5.092)	0.489**	25.933
5.	Textiles	12.603** (8.612)	0.064 (0.755)	0.021	0.571
6.	Clothing & Footwear	14.337** (11.492)	–0.015 (–0.218)	0.002	0.047
7.	Leather, Leather Goods and Fur	15.307** (5.903)	0.072 (0.482)	0.008	0.023

(Contd.)

Table 4.2 : (Contd.)

1	2	3	4	5	6
8.	Bricks, Pottery, Glass, Ceramics, etc.	16.545** (14.919)	–0.049 (–0.457)	0.013	0.209
9.	Paper Printing & Publishing	10.964** (8.897)	0.281** (3.916)	0.362**	15.337
	CONSUMER GOODS SECTOR	12.557** (18.577)	0.197** (5.014)	0.482**	25.144
10.	Metal Manufacture	11.664** (6.207)	–0.052 (–0.478)	0.008	0.229
11.	Chemicals & Allied Industries	10.969** (8.035)	0.297** (3.742)	0.341**	14.003
	BASIC GOODS SECTOR	10.665** (7.710)	0.268** (3.334)	0.291**	11.121
12.	Vehicles	14.189** (5.026)	–0.365* (–2.225)	0.154*	4.952
13.	Electrical Engineering including Electronics	11.731** (16.768)	0.385** (9.452)	0.767**	89.344
14.	Non-Electrical Engineering	14.026** (11.564)	0.005 (0.066)	0.0002	0.0043
15.	Metal Goods Not elsewhere specified	17.871** (13.529)	–0.203* (–2.647)	0.206*	7.008
16.	Ship Building and Marine Engineering	7.339* (2.172)	–0.527* (–2.578)	0.197*	6.649
	CAPITAL GOODS SECTOR	13.772** (8.527)	0.013 (0.148)	0.008	0.022
17.	Other Manufacturing Industries (INTERMEDIARY GOODS SECTOR)	11.933** (8.424)	0.178* (2.157)	0.147*	4.656
	WHOLE MANUFACTURING SECTOR	12.452** (12.379)	0.153* (2.623)	0.203*	6.885

Source : Table 4.1

Notes :
1. Figures in Brackets are *t* values.
2. ** Indicates that estimate is significant at 1% level.
3. * Indicates that estimate is significant at 5% level.
4. Bricks, Pottery, Glass, Ceramics covers the period upto 1976–77 only while other industries cover the period 1960–61 to 1988–89.

Estimates of Trend Coefficients for U.K. Manufacturing Industries

The Model of time trend coefficient fitted for Indian Manufacturing industries is fitted for U.K. industries also. The Linear model fittted as follows[1]:

$$P = \alpha + \beta t + e$$

Where P is profit rate, α and β are parameters, t is time and e is the error term. The results of this model fitted to Profitability series of U.K. Manufacturing industries are presented in Table 4.2. Following results are derived.

1. It is observed from Tale 4.2 that the Linear Model of time Trend of Profitability has turned out to be a "good fit" in case of Nine out of Seventeen U.K. Manufacturing Industries, i.e., in case of 52.9% of total industries studied here. This is revealed by the value of R^2, the coefficient of determination.

2. Six out of these 9 industries enjoyed a strong rising tendency in rates of profit over the study period. This is obvious from the positive sign and statistically significant value of β, the time trend coefficient for them. The industries with rising profitability are Food, Tobacco, Paper Printing and Publishing (Consumers Goods Sector), Chemical and Allied Industries (Basic Goods Sector), Electrical Engineering Including Electronics (Capital Goods Sector) and Other Manufacturing Industries (Intermediary Goods Sector).

3. The positive value of β, the time trend coefficient, implies that profitability of the industry rises over time as it is positively related to time. It may further be noted from Table 4.2 that β assumes different values for different industries from 0.178 for Other Manufacturing industries to 0.385 for Electrical Engineering including Electronics over the study period. In other words, profitability of different manufacturing industries of U.K. increased at

1. For details see Section III of Chapter III.

different rates over the period 1960-61 to 1988-89.

4. Table 4.2 further reveals that 3 industries, viz., Vehicles. Metal Goods Not Elsewhere Specified and Ship Building and Marine Engineering, suffered a set back to their profitability, as β, the time trend coefficient assumes, statistically significant negative values like –0.365, –0.203, and –0.507 respectively, indicating that their profitability declined at different rates over this period.

5. No definite trend could be observed in case of Eight U.K. industries as the regression results are statistically non-significant.

6. R^2, the coefficient of determination provides the degree of fitness of the model. It was found statistically significant for the industries having rising trending profitability and also varies in value from 0.147 for Other Manufacturing industries to 0.767 for Electrical Engineering including Electronics. This indicates that time explains rise in profitability of U.K. Manufacturing Industries in different degrees.

7. In case of industries with declining profit rate over time, R^2 assumed different values, e.g., 0.15 for Vehicles, 0.206 for Metal Goods Not Elsewhere Specified and 0.197 for ship-building and Marine Engineering, implying thereby that the fall in profitability is explained by time in different degrees.

8. In case of four out of the five sectors (except Capital Goods Sector) the Linear Bivariate Model of Time Trend has proved to be "good fit" as both R^2, the coefficient of determination and β, the time trend coefficient, are found to be statistically significant. It is further observed from Table 4.2 that β assumes positive and statistically significant values for all these four sectors and varies in value from 0.153 for Whole Manufacturing Sector 0.268 for Basic Goods Sector, indicating that profit rate rises in different degrees in these sectors over the study period.

9. R^2, the coefficient of determination also assumes different

value, e.g., 0147 for Intermediary Goods Sector (Other Manufacturing Industries) and 0.482 for Consumer Goods Sector, implying that time explains variations in rates of profit of these sectors in different degrees over the study period. The results are found to be statistically non-significant for Capital Goods Sector.

Dispersions in Rates of Profit of U.K. Manufacturing Industries

This part of the Chapter relates to dispersions in profitability series of U.K. Manufacturing Industries over the period 1960-61 to 1988-89. Table 4.3 summarises the estimates of mean, standard deviation and coefficient of variation for each of the profitability series for these industries over the study period. Following conclusions are drawn from the Table 4.3.

Table 4.3 : Industrywise Variation in Profitability of U.K. Manufacturing Sector : 1960–61 to 1988–89

Ind. S.No.	*Industry*	*Mean*	*S.D.*	*C.V.*
1.	Food	16.3	2.5	0.151
2.	Drink	14.4	1.8	0.123
3.	Timber Furniture	16.7	6.6	0.393
4.	Tobacco	17.8	3.8	0.212
5.	Textiles	13.6	3.7	0.276
6.	Clothing & Footwear	14.1	3.2	0.224
7.	Leather, Leather Goods and Fur	16.4	6.6	0.402
8.	Bricks, Pottery, Glass, Ceramics, etc.	16.1	2.1	0.128
9.	Paper Printing & Publishing	15.2	3.9	0.257
	CONSUMER GOODS SECTOR	15.5	2.4	0.153
10.	Metal Manufacture	10.9	4.8	0.439
11.	Chemical & Allied Industries	15.4	4.3	0.276
	BASIC GOODS SECTOR	14.7	4.2	0.283
12.	Vehicles	8.7	7.8	0.893

(Contd.)

Table 4.3 : (Contd.)

Ind. S.No.	*Industry*	*Mean*	*S.D.*	*C.V.*
13.	Electrical Engineering including Electronics.	17.5	3.7	0.210
14.	Non-Electrical Engineering	14.1	3.1	0.218
15.	Metal Goods Not Elsewhere Specified	14.8	3.7	0.253
16.	Ship Building & Marine Engineering	–0.3	+9.5	–35.492
	CAPITAL GOODS SECTOR	14.0	4.1	0.292
17.	Other Manufacturing Industries (INTERMEDIARY GOODS SECTOR)	14.6	3.9	0.266
	WHOLE MANUFACTURING SECTOR	14.8	2.9	0.193

Source : Table 4.1

Notes : 1. Mean = $\overline{P} = \frac{\sum_{j=1}^{n} P_j}{n}$ where P_j = Rate of Profits for j^{th} industry.

n = Number of years.

2. S.D. = Standard Deviation = $\sigma = \sqrt{\frac{\Sigma(P_j - \overline{P})^2}{n}}$

3. C.V. = Coefficient of Variation = $\overline{P}/\sigma$

1. Table 4.3 reveals that, on an average, Tobacco industry enjoyed the highest profit rate of 17.8% while Ship Building and Marine Engineering Industry, suffered the lowest and negative rate of profit (–0.3%) over the study period.

2. Mean rate of Profit for the Whole Manufacturing Sector is observed to be 14.8% and only Consumers Goods Sector had the mean profit rate (15.5%), above this sector, while all other sectors had it below the Whole Manufacturing Sector.

3. Out of 17 industries examined for U.K. Manufacturing Sector, nine industries, on an average, enjoyed rate of profit above that enjoyed by Whole Manufacturing Sector, while seven had below it. These 9 industries are, Food,

Timber Furniture, Tobacco, Leather, Leather Goods and Fur, Bricks, Pottery, Glass/Ceramics etc. Paper Printing and Publishing (6 out of 9 Consumer Goods Sector Industries) Chemical and Allied Industries (Basic Goods Sector) Electrical Engineering Including Electronics, Metal Goods Not Elsewhere Specified (2 out of 5 Capital Goods Sector Industries).

It is interesting to note here that majority of industries belonging to Consumer Goods Sector (66.7%), and 50% of Basic Goods Sector enjoyed, on an average . profit rate above the Whole Manufacturing Sector during the study period.

Finally, it is interesting to observe from Table 4.3 that variation in mean rate of profit for industries belonging to Consumer Goods Sector are very less while in case of Basic and Capital Goods Industries, these are very high.

Table 5.3 also presents the estimates of standard deviation and coefficient of variation for each of the profitability series for U.K. Manufacturing industries, providing absolute and relative variations respectively in actual values of profit rate series from its mean value. Following observations are made.

1. Table 4.3 reveals that Drink industry experienced the lowest variations in its profitability series with coefficient of variation equal to 0.123, while Ship Building & Marine Engineering, with lowest and negative mean profit rate (–0.3%) suffered from largest variations. coefficient of variation assuming value equal of –35.492.

2. Consumers Goods Sector with coefficient of Variation being lowest (C.V. = 0.153) experienced lowest variations while Capital Goods Sector had the largest variations (C.V. =0.292) during the study period.

3. The arbitrary division of industries in Relatively Stable, (C.V. upto 0.250), Moderately fluctuating (C.V. lying between 0.251 and 0.500), Highly fluctuating (C.V. lying between 0.501 to 0.750) and Erratically fluctuating (C.V. equal to or above 0.751), reveals that seven U.K. indus-

tries (41.2% of total 17 industries) viz., Food, Drink, Tobacco, Clothing & Footwear; Bricks, Pottery, Glass, Ceramics, etc. (5 out of 9 Consumer Goods Industries), Electrical Engineering Including Electronics; Non-Electrical Engineering (2 out of 5 Capital Goods Industries) experienced relatively stable profitability series, while Eight industries (47.1%) of total industries examined) had moderately fluctuating profit rates. Industries having moderate fluctuations in profitability series are Timber Furniture, Textiles, Leather, Leather Goods and Fur; Paper Printing and Publishing (4 out of 9 Consumer Goods Industries) Metal Manufacture; Chemical & Allied Industries (both the Basic Goods Industries), Metal Goods Not Elsewhere Specified (2 out of 5 Capital Goods Industries), and Other manufacturing Industries (Intermediary Goods Sector).

Vehicles and Ship Building and Marine Engineering were the two industries which experienced Erratically fluctuating series of profit rate over the study period.

4. Amongst the sectors, the Consumers Goods Sector had lowest variations (V.C. = 0.153) in profit rate series while the Capital Goods Sector suffered from largest Variations (C.V. = 0.292). The Consumer Goods Sector and Whole Manufacturing Sector enjoyed Relatively Stable profit rate series while Basic Capital and Intermediary Goods Sector had Moderately fluctuating series.

In short, six U.K. Manufacturing industries experienced rising trend in profitability over study period while 3 had strong tendency for decline in profit rate series over the study period. No definite Trend could be observed in case of 8 industries. Degree of variation in profitability of these industries varies over time. More over, majority of U.K. industries had relatively or moderately fluctuating profitability series while only two had erratic fluctuations in these series.

5
Profitability Trends and Business Cycles in Indian Manufacturing

Importance of the Study of Profitability Trends and Business Cycles in India

One of the most important criticisms put forth against market economies based on free enterprise system relates to the existence of business cycles causing cyclical fluctuations in economic activities. These economic fluctuations exert tremendous influence on the economy, especially on the rate of return and stock of capital of various concerns in industries.

Business cycles or alternating periods of prosperity and depression greatly affect almost all the concerns in the industry. Inspite of the fact that business cycles are entirely beyond the control of the manager of an individual business concern, the knowledge about their presence and the surrounding economic conditions enables the concern to avoid as many losses as possible and to avail as many opportunities of making profits as possible.

Endogenous factors (factors within the control of the economy, like, capital formation, inventory accumulation, rate of interest, money supply, government activities to stabilize the economy through maintenance of level of output, employment, prices etc., as well as exogenous factors (which are outside the control of the economy), like wars, innovations, population changes, technological changes, etc., exert influence on business cycles.

The period of business cycles varies from 2 to 3 years (Kitchen Cycles) to 10 years (Juglar Cycles), or, may even prolong upto 50 years (Kondratieff Cycles). It may, however, be noted that the turning points of business cycles, viz., peak or trongh, need not affect all the industries at the same time and with the same intensity. Some sectors are hit first by recovery or recession, which then cumulatively spreads to other sectors of the economy.

A manager of a concern who is well-equipped with the knowledge of business cycles can easily face the period of peak and the following downward swing by holding down the inventories, reducing the plant and equipment expansion to the minimum, and, extending the credit carefully. This would help him reduce the losses to minimum. If the first faces recovery, he may behave in opposite manner to earn large profits. In short, knowledge of the presence of various phases of business cycles, would enable the manager to suffer no or minimum losses or enjoy high profits.

Though business cycles exert tremendous influence on rate on profit and stock of capital, this has remained a highly neglected field of research, particularly in terms of comparative analysis of two or more countries. Hence, an attempt has been made in this and the following chapter to examine the influence of business cycles on profitability ratios of Indian and U. K. Manufacturing industries respectively, during the period 1960-61 to 1988-89.

It has been observed in Chapter III that 8 out of 19 Indian Manufacturing industries[1] suffered from strong tendency in profit rate to decline over the study period, alongwith Consumer, and Basic Goods sectors and Whole manufacturing sector,

1. Please refer to Chater 3.

while results of time trend regression analysis were statistically non-significant for remaining 11 industries and 2 sectors. The industries experiencing fall in profitability are Grains and Pulses, Silk Rayon and Woollen Textiles, Medicines and Pharmaceutical Preparations, Aluminium, Cement, Electrical Machinery, Apparatus and Appliances, errors/Non-Ferrous Metal Products and Jute Textiles.

The "Time Trend Analysis" of profitability throws light on strong tendencies of rates of profit to move in a particular direction, e.g., a fall in case of above mentioned Indian manufacturing industries. However, factors other than those related to trend exert influence on the time series data. Each of these factors represents a well-defined type of economic change. Since business cycles are one amongst these factors, these need to be isolated from the trend.

Various economists have separately made attempts to detect business cycles in various countries, like I. Mintz for W. Germany and U.S.A. (59, 60, 1969, 1974 respectively), M. Friedman and Schwartz (31) for U.S.A., V.S. Chibre (18, 1982) L.A. Rede (81, 1988) for India. However, no author has undertaken a comparative study of profitability trends and business cycle in manufacturing sector of two different countries over a fairly long period of 29 years, as is undertaken in this study.

Though the regressicn coefficients of time trend analysis for above given 8 industries are BLUE (Best, /Linear, Unbiased, Efficient) giving us a "good fit", the time series data comprise of four economic changes, viz., secular trend, seasonal variations, business cycles and random or erratic fluctuations which intermingle with above changes. This requires isolation of these economic changes by decomposing the series. Following methodology is used for this purpose.

Methodology

It has been observed that the cyclical fluctuations show wide variations in the length of the cycle and also in the amplitude of the variations. Hence, deriving one method which can be applied uniformly to all the studies, has proved to be a difficult task. Business volume expands and contract in an oscillating movement, that varies greatly in the time required to make a complete cycle. Due to this irregular nature of the cycles it becomes difficult to find an average cycle to represent an effect on the series. However, cyclical fluctuations can be isolated from the trend of the time series, so that, purely secular trend in the series be derived.

As observed earlier, 8 out of 19 Indian Manufacturing industries suffered from decline in profit rate over the period 1960-61 to 1988-89, i.e. 29 years. Majority of these industries belonged to Basic (2 industries) and Capital (2 out of 4 industries) Goods Sectors, while a few belonged to Consumers Goods sector 3 out of 9 industries) and Intermediary Goods Sector (1 out of 3). Most of these industries (except Cement and Jute Textiles are of recent origin and belong to chemical and engineering group of industries.

As explained earlier, the trend analysis of profit rates contains the business cycles which need to be separated. The most commonly used method of isolating trend and business cycles in a series is to express the actual data for profit rate as a percentage of trend value for each year for each industry. The business cycles thus located are termed as deviation cycles. Another methodis to compare the rate of growth of actual profit rate to that of its trend value. These are termed growth cycles (Chitra, 18, 1982). The present study is confirmed to the exploration of deviation cycles in profit rates of manufacturing industries in India and U.K. The logic underlying the above said methodology is to assume, that, the cyclical movement is essentially independent of the trend, and that, the forces making for cyclical fluctuations, have approximately the same relative effect on the series, regardless of the level of the trend. Appendix Table 5-A and Appendix Table 6-A, represent the ratios of Actual to trend value of profit rate for each industry over the study periodfor India and U.K. Manufacturing sectors respectively.

Before we taken up the analysis on detection of business cycles, it is essential to define them. A business cycle is made up of four economic phases, viz., recession, depression, revival (recovery) and boom (prosperity). "Burns and Mitchell (15,

1946), defined business cycles as, :Business cycles are a type of fluctuations found in the aggregate economic activity of nations that organize their work mainly in business enterprise: a cycle consists of expansions occurring at about the same time in many economic atrocities, followed by similar general recessions, contractions and revivals which merge into the expansions phase of the next cycle, this sequence of change is recurrent but not periodic."

In the world of non-perfection, where changes are bound to affect the whole economy, and where, no change would be expected, the first impact of change would be on the rates of profit which would ultimately affect the distribution of wealth and the growth of economy. Stigler (98,1963) therefore comments, "And in the opposite world, where no change would ever be expected the first impact of every change would be on the rates of return: every surge of demand would find the industry unprepared and its prices and profit rates would rise; every cessation of demand would find the industry over expanded and its output selling at distress prices." This implies that, in the dynamic world, an industry has to cope with a number of forces such as: changing consumers' incomes; competition with domestic and foreign producers; changing prices of inputs; discovery of new resources, techniques of production and new products, etc. All these changes and the adjustments made to them are portrayed in two basic data of each industry, viz., its stock of capital and the rate of return on this capital.

In sum, a business cycle comprises of four economic phases, viz., recession, depression, revival and room. Imbalance between aggregate demand and supply of commodity results into economic fluctuations. Recession indicates a situation of glut in the market with deficiency of aggregate demand in relation to aggregate supply and leads to initial stages of low economic activities, leading further to depression or lowest level of economic activities. Hence, outputs, prices, rates of interest, employment, incomes, investment, saving, all shrink to lowest possible level during depression. On the other hand, revival is an initial stage of expansion of economic activities (mentioned above) which results into boom or prosperity and cause the upward rise in economy activities, taking these to highest level. The lowest level of economic activity or depression is called "Trough," while the highest level or boom is called" Peak" of the business cycle. These alternating phases of business cycle are quite pervasive, self-propelling, and recurrent, though these need not be periodic.

The next step after defining the business cycles is to translate these four phases of business cycles in terms of operational definitions. This is achieved by estimating first the deviation cycle via working out the ratio of actual to trend value of profit rate (rounded to second decimal place) for each industry over the study period [see Appendix Table 5–A and 6–A]. If the value of the ratio is less than "one", or, "100%", it indicates a situation of low levels of economic activities and if it is greater than "one" or "100%", it reflects high levels of economic activities.

The next step undertaken then is that of identification of turning points: i.e., troughs and peaks, of individual deviation cycles for each industry over the study period of 29 years. Depending upon the change of direction, i.e., rise or fall, the troughs and peaks in each series were located through inspection. When deviations remained same before showing a change of direction, the year corresponding to the last of the equal values is considered as the turning point.

A period preceding "trough" is the termed as the period of "Contraction", while that following the "Trough" is named " Expansion". Thus, phase of recession is denoted by contraction, while trough indicates depression. Similarly, expansion represents revival while peak shows boom or prosperity. Thus, a period between two troughs or two peaks reveals a complete business cycle and covers all the four phases.

Detection of Deviation Cycles in Indian Manufacturing

Appendix Table 5–A presents the estimates of ratio of actual profit rate to trend value of profit rate for each Indian manufacturing industry and sector over the period 1960-61 to 1988-89.On the basis of thorough inspection of this table, following observations are made.

(A) Detection of Phases of Contraction and Expansion

(i) Indian manufacturing sector experienced period of contraction for "seven" times during the study period with average period of contraction for the whole Manufacturing sector being 2.800 years.

(ii) The period of expansion experienced during the same period was also for seven times with the average period of expansion being 3.00 years (Please refer to Table 5.1).

Table 5.1 : Periods of Contraction and Expansion in Indian Manufacturing Section

Periods	Years						
Contraction	1960–62	1963–64	1967–69	1972–73	1975–77	1980–83	1985–87
Expansion	1962–63	1964–67	1969–72	1973–75	1977–80	1983–85	1987–89

Source : Appendix Table 5–A.

(iii) A period is called as period of contraction/expansion (denoted by fall or rise in the series) when majority of industries are experiencing contraction/expansion in a particular period. A further look in Table 5.1 reveals that both contactionary and expansionary period varied between 1 to 3 years. however. the former was dominated by 2 years' period while the latter by 3 years' period.

(iv) Table 5.2 presents the distribution of Indian manufacturing industries by sectors. experiencing the periods of contracting and expansion. A close examination of Table 5.2 reveals that majority industries belonging to Consumer, Basic. Capital, Intermediary and Whole Manufacturing sectors underwent a phase of contacting during these periods (Except for 1963-64).

(v) Table 5.2 also reveals that (except for the period 1962-63) majority industries belong to all these sectors experienced expansionary phase during the periods of expansion.

Table 5.2 : Number of Industries in Contraction and Expansion Phase in the Ratio of Actual to Trend Value of Profit Rate in Indian Manufacturing Industries : 1960–61 to 1988–89

Total No.	Period of Contraction							SECTORS	Period of Expansion						
of Industries	1960 –62	1963 –64	1967 –69	1972 –73	1975 –77	1980 –83	1985 –87		1962 –63	1964 –67	1969 –72	1973 –75	1977 –80	1983 –85	1987 –89
9	7	5	8	7	7	8	7	CONSUMER GOODS SECTOR	3	9	8	6	9	5	6
3	3	2	3	2	2	3	2	BASIC GOODS SECTOR	2	3	3	3	3	1	1
4	2	3	4	4	3	4	3	CAPITAL GOODS SECTOR	4	3	3	4	4	2	4
3	2	3	3	2	3	3	1	INTERMEDIARY GOODS SECTOR	1	2	2	1	3	2	2
19	14	13	18	15	15	18	13	WHOLE MANU-FACTURING SECTOR	10	17	16	14	19	10	13

Note : 1. Total number of industries covered in Whole Manufacturing Sector is 19 upto 1980–81 and 16 between 1981–82 and 1988–89.

2. Total number of Industries covered under Consumer Goods Sector is 9 and in Basic Goods Sector 3 upto 1980–81 and 6 and 2 respectively after 1980–81.

(vi) Observations (iv) and (v) given above lead us to conclude strongly regarding the existence of phases of contraction and expansion depicted in Table 5.1

(B) Periodicity of Business Cycle in Indian Manufacturing

Business cycles may be periodic or non-periodic. The estimates presented in Table 5.3 reveal that business cycles are non-periodic as regards Indian manufacturing sector. The periodicity of business cycles is examined by examining the deviations in profitability of each industry over the study period. As mentioned earlier, a business cycle is completed when movement from trough to peak and again to next trough occurs, or, movement from peak-trough-teak takes place. Since these completed cycles have no identical trough-peak-trough period or peak-trough-peak periods, these are non-periodic. Table 5.3 reveals the average duration and amplitude of deviation cycles in Indian manufacturing over the period 1960-61 to 1988-89. Following observations are made.

Table 5.3 : Periodicity of Business Cycles in Indian Manufacturing for the Ratio of Actual to Trend Value of Profit Rate

Industry	*Average No. of years of TPT cycles*	*No. of complete business cycles*	*Average no. of years of PTP cycles*	*No. of complete business cycles*
1. Grains and Pulses	3.40	5	3.20	5
2. Edible Vegetable & Hydrogenated Oils	3.13	8	3.00	7
3. Sugar	4.33	6	4.00	5
4. Tobacco	2.71	7	2.67	6
5. Cotton Textiles	3.57	7	3.38	8
6. Silk, Rayon and Woollen Textiles	4.00	6	4.17	6

(Contd.)

Table 5.3 : (Contd.)

Industry	*Average No. of years of TPT cycles*	*No. of complete business cycles*	*Average no. of years of PTP cycles*	*No. of complete business cycles*
7. Medicines and Pharmaceutical Preparations	5.00	5	4.60	5
8. Pottery, China, Earthenware and Structural Clay Products	4.60	5	4.33	6
9. Paper and Paper Products	4.33	6	4.33	6
CONSUMER GOODS SECTOR	4.17	6	4.00	6
10. Aluminium	3.80	5	4.00	4
11. Basic Industrial Chemicals	4.80	5	4.80	5
12. Cement	3.86	7	3.33	6
BASIC GOODS SECTOR	3.25	8	3.25	8
13. Transport Equipment	4.00	6	3.71	7
14. Electrical Machinery, Apparatus and Appliances	6.00	3	6.25	4
15. Machinery (Other tan Transport and Electrical Equipment)	2.89	9	2.89	9
16. Ferrous/Non-Ferrous Metal Products	3.38	8	3.57	7
CAPITAL GOODS SECTOR	4.50	4	4.80	5
17. Jute Textiles	2.89	9	2.89	9
18. Other Chemical Products	2.78	9	2.89	9
19. Rubber & Rubberr Products	6.50	2	2.00	1
INTERMEDIARY GOODS SECTOR	3.00	9	3.13	8
WHOLE MANUFACTURING SECTOR	6.25	4	6.00	4

Source : Appendix Table V-A.

Note : Average number of years of TPT/PTP cycles are derived by dividing total number of years under TPT/PTP respectively by the number of complete cycles under these.

(i) Table 5.3 shows that majority of Indian industries belonging to Consumer Goods Sector and Basic Goods Sector experienced complete 5 or 6 Trough-Peak-Trough (TPT), or, Peak-Trough-Peak (PTP) cycles, while majority of industries belonging to Capital Goods Sector and Intermediary Goods Sector had complete 8 or 9 years TPT/PTP cycles, during the study period.

(ii) Rubber and Rubber Products and Electrical Machinery, Apparatus and Appliances had minimum complete 2 and 3 TPT cycles respectively and 1 and 4 cycles respectively, while Machinery (Other than Transport and Electrical Equipment) Jute Textiles, Other Chemical Products experienced 9 complete TPT/PTP cycles while Vegetable and Hydrogenated Oils and Ferrous/Non-Ferrous Metal Products had 8 complete TPT and 7 complete PTP cycles.

(iii) The Whole Manufacturing sector and Capital Goods Sector had complete 4 TPT cycles while these had complete 4 and 5 PTP cycles respectively. The Consumer goods Sector experienced 6 Completed TPT/PTP Cycles, while Basic and Intermediary Goods Sector had complete 8 and 9 TPT cycles respectively and 8 PTP cycles each.

(iv) All industries and sectors except Electrical Machinery, Apparatus and Appliances and Rubber and Rubber Products industries and Capital Goods Sector (for TPT cycles), experienced larger completed TPT/PTP cycles in comparison with respective sectors during the study period.

(v) The average duration of TPT cycles ranged between 2.71 years for Tobacco to 6.5 years for Rubber and Rubber Products, while for PTP cycles it varied from 2.00 years for Rubber and Rubber Products to 6.25 years for Electrical Machinery, Apparatus and Appliances.

(vi) It may further be noted from Table 5.3 that majority of industries belonging to Consumer, Basic and Intermediary Goods Sectors experienced average duration of TPT/PTP cycles below or around 4.33 years while only 5 industries and Capital Goods Sector and Whole Manufacturing Sector had above it.

In short the number of business cycles in Indian manufacturing industries between 1960-61 to 1988-89, for complete cycles was 5 to 6 or 8 to 9 TPT/PTP cycles, with average duration ranging between 2 to 6.50 years.

(C) Amplitude of Business Cycles in Indian Manufacturing

The results showing the amplitude of business cycles in rate of profit in Indian Manufacturing are presented in Table 5.4. This provides information on rise and fall during expansionary and contractionary phases of complete TPT/PTP cycles over the period 1960-61 to 1988-89.

The figures for average amplitude of deviation cycles over the entire period for each industry are presented in columns 2 and 3 of Table 5.4. These are computed for the whole series over the study period by taking simple average of rise and fall of actual profit rate from its trends value and are worked out for all the industries. If actual profit rate exceeds the trend value of profit rate it denotes rise while if the former is smaller than the latter, it indicates fall. Following conclusions are drawn:

(i) Table 5.4 (columns 2 and 3) reveals that variation of actual profit rate from its trend value in case of rise ranges between 14.88% for Tobacco to 260.47% for Jute Textiles. As regards the deviation of actual profit rate from its trend value in case of fall, it ranges between 15.06% for Medicines and Pharmaceutical Preparations to 248.8% for Jute Textiles over the study period.

(ii) A further look into columns 2 and 3 of Table 5.3 reveals that Whole Manufacturing sector had deviation of actual profit rate from its trend value to the tune of 17.78% for rise and 14.37% in case of fall. All other sectors had these deviations being larger than the Whole Manufacturing Sector (except for Basic goods Sector in case of fall).

(iii) Another important observation made from columns 2 and 3 of Table 5.3 is that most of the agro-based industries (except Tobacco), viz., Grains and Pulses, Edible Vegetable and Hydrogenated Oils, Sugar, Cotton Textiles, Silk-

Table 5.4 : Average Amplitude of Business Cycle and Average Amplitude per year of Series of Ratio of Actual to Trend Value of Profit Rate in Indian Manufacturing Industries : 1960–61 to 1988–89

Industry	*Average Amplitude of Business Cycles (%)*		*Average Amplitudes per TPT Cycle (%age point)*		*Average Amplitude per Year for the series (%age point)*	
	Rise	Fall	Rise	Fall	Rise	Fall
(1)	(2)	(3)	(4)	(5)	(6)	(7)
1. Grains and Pulses	104.89	70.58	167.18	138.02	74.21	128.38
2. Edible Vegetable and Hydrogenated Oils	35.34	33.09	71.35	68.94	47.05	42.32
3. Sugar	24.66	43.05	101.77	140.23	63.04	41.32
4. Tobacco	14.88	16.33	26.43	23.01	20.34	19.73
5. Cotton Textiles	60.66	32.41	61.65	70.74	32.12	37.07
6. Silk-Rayon and Woollen Textiles	21.66	24.49	53.38	47.57	32.20	29.90
7. Medicines and Pharmaceutical Preparations	17.79	15.06	26.92	28.84	12.36	12.80
8. Potter-China, Earthenware & Structural Clay Products	38.54	35.87	36.55	46.10	17.67	14.39
9. Paper and Paper Products	50.45	31.96	52.30	68.15	26.01	30.61
CONSUMER GOODS SECTOR	23.42	19.64	29.40	35.55	12.20	22.84
10. Aluminium	33.74	24.10	76.46	85.16	47.39	51.04
11. Basic Industrial Chemicals	25.79	16.01	25.70	37.04	16.11	16.58

Contd.

Table 5.4 : (Contd.)

Industry	*Average Amplitude of Business Cycles* (%)		*Average Amplitudes per TPT Cycle* (*%age point*)		*Average Amplitude per Year for the* (*%age point*)	
	Rise	Fall	Rise	Fall	Rise	Fall
(1)	(2)	(3)	(4)	(5)	(6)	(7)
12. Cement	46.92	35.49	75.74	82.46	32.21	40.51
BASIC GOODS SECTOR	20.10	8.14	18.30	22.51	12.55	12.92
13. Transport Equipment	24.78	21.36	46.21	52.79	25.49	15.31
14. Electrical Machinery, Apparatus & Appl.	22.26	21.09	40.25	42.94	17.63	12.39
15. Machinery (Other than Transport & Electrical Equipments)	33.53	33.51	56.42	53.07	40.93	47.43
16. Ferrous/Non-Ferrous Metal Products	46.49	33.35	73.51	52.88	50.69	37.15
CAPITAL GOODS SECTOR	20.59	20.65	30.94	39.58	14.59	13.56
17. Jute Textiles	260.47	248.84	159.87	175.41	693.54	674.78
18. Other Chemical Products	15.81	48.70	52.09	49.05	30.55	35.18
19. Rubber and Rubber Products	34.31	21.51	0.10	29.50	0.10	4.39
INTERMEDIARY GOODS SECTOR	34.72	28.13	67.59	68.63	46.53	41.19
WHOLE MANUFACTURING SECTOR	17.78	14.37	28.08	39.63	8.79	19.55

Note : For details of estimates see the text.

Rayon and Woollen Textiles (only for fall), Paper and Paper Products and Jute Textiles had both rise and fall above that of their respective sectors and the Whole Manufacturing Sector. Moreover except Tobacco, Silk-Ray on and Woollen Textiles and Medicine and Pharmaceutical Preparation for rise, all industries belonging to Consumer Goods Sector experienced both rise and fall above Consumer Goods Sector and Whole Manufacturing Sector.

(iv) Similarly all the industries belonging to Basic, Capital and Intermediary goods Sector (except Rubber and Rubber Products), had both rise and fall above their respective sectors and all industries had it above Whole Manufacturing Sector.

(v) The average amplitude for each deviation cycle during contraction and expansion phases is calculated on the basis of the levels of peaks and troughs for deviation cycles. The estimates for these are presented in columns 4 and 5 of Table 5.4. It is observed from column 4 that the average speed of rise ranged between 0.1 percentage point for Rubber and Rubber Products to 159.87 percentage point in case of Jute Textiles, while, average speed of fall ranged between 23.01 percentage points for Tobacco to 175.1 percentage points in case of Jute Textiles (see Column 5).

(vi) The fluctuations recorded for Basic Goods Sector were lowest for both the rise (18.30 percentage points) and fall (22.51 percentage points). Except Basic Goods Sector, all the sectors had fluctuations above the whole manufacturing sector as regards the rise while these had below it in case of all (except Intermediary goods sector).

(vii) Except Tobacco, Medicines and Pharmaceutical Preparations, Basic Industrial Chemicals and Rubber and Rubber Products industries, all other industries had very high fluctuations in both the rise and fall. (Columns 4 and 5).

(viii) Columns 6 and 7 of Table 5.4 indicate average amplitude per year for the average speed of rise or fall of the series and is computed by taking the simple averages of the per year amplitude in the relevant phases. Hence, a simple relationship between the estimates of columns 4-5 and 6-7 can not be expected (Chitra, 18, 1982). The estimates of columns 6 and 7 confirm the conclusions drawn above.

The per year amplitude for rise ranged between 0.10 percentage points for Rubber and Rubber Products to 693.5 percentage points in case of Jute Textiles, while the same two industries experienced a fall ranging between 4.39 percentage point for former and 67.78 percentage point for latter.

(ix) It is further observed from columns 6 and 7 of Table 5.4 that Tobacco, Medicines and Pharmaceutical Preparations, Pottery, China-Earthenware and Structural Clay Products, Basic Industrial Chemicals, Transport Equipment, Electrical Machinery, Apparatus and Appliances and Rubber and Rubber Products, i.e. 7 out of 19 (36.8% industries) industries experienced relatively less fluctuations per year compared to other industries.

(x) The per year amplitude of rise was lowest (8.79) per centage points) in case of Whole Manufacturing Sector and highest for Intermediary Goods Sector (46.53 percentage points). As regards fall, per year amplitude ranged between 12.92 percentage points for Basic Goods Sector and 41.19 percentage point for Intermediary goods Sector.

In short, Consumer, Capital and Basic Goods Sectors have been observed to be relatively less fluctuating while Intermediary Goods Sector is widely fluctuating with respect to rise and fall of profit rates over the study period.

Conclusions

On the basis of above given analysis following broad conclusions are derived:

(i) Indian manufacturing industries experienced 7 phases of both expansion and contraction during the period 1960-

61 to 1988-89, i.e, 29 years.

(ii) Majority of industries belonging to all the sectors faced trough during contraction phase and peak during expansion phase.

(iii) Majority of industries had complete 5 to 6 or 8 to 9 TPT/ PTP cycles with average duration ranging between 2 to 6.50 years.

(iv) Majority of industries belonging to Consumer, Basic and Intermediary Goods Sectors had average duration of TPT/ PTP cycles below or around 4.33 years, while a few had above it.

(v) It is further observed that as regards the amplitude of business cycles, the agro-based industries had larger fluctuations in rise as well as well.

(vi) Majority of industries belonging to Consumer, Basic and Capital Goods sector experienced relatively smaller fluctuations while those belonging to Intermediary Goods Sector had wide fluctuations.

(vii) Since the study is confined to private corporate sector of Indian Industries, that too covering only medium and large companies, its conclusions with respect to basic and capital goods industries need to be treated carefully because these have been predominantly in the public sector.

APPENDIX TABLE 5–A : Ratio of Actual Profit Rate and Trend Value of Profit Rate for Indian Manufacturing Industries : 1960–61 to 1988–89 (per cent)

Year	Grains and pulses	Edible Vegetable & Hydrogenated Oil	Sugar	Tobacco	Cotton Textiles	Silk-Rayon & Woollen Textiles	Medicines & Pharmaceuticals preparations	Pottery-China, Earthernware & Structural Clay Products	Paper & Paper Products	CONSUMER SECTOR	Aluminium	Basic Industrial Chemicals	Cement	BASIC GOODS SECTOR
	1	2	3	4	5	6	7	8	9		10	11	12	
1960–61	123.1	95.1	122.9	85.5	132.6	98.7	113.8	68.4	90.1	104.5	103.3	104.9	73.7	90.0
1961–62	84.2	71.3	93.6	78.0	146.0	83.8	72.6	116.3	84.4	103.4	84.3	98.0	52.7	89.9
1962–63	70.0	68.3	76.2	99.6	86.3	80.1	69.3	118.1	88.5	78.3	90.3	86.1	117.8	96.6
1963–64	96.5	57.2	122.0	75.2	94.6	79.8	87.5	96.5	81.9	85.6	123.1	83.2	109.5	96.0
1964–65	175.0	106.0	128.0	107.9	96.2	63.6	97.3	55.4	67.7	90.3	134.9	97.7	111.9	105.9
1965–66	116.2	109.1	131.4	124.6	42.5	93.3	123.3	75.4	54.5	79.7	94.4	87.1	119.3	96.5
1966–67	133.4	144.8	96.3	98.8	75.0	116.6	121.7	69.7	66.0	93.2	86.6	96.3	155.9	104.9
1967–68	77.6	49.2	56.3	122.0	53.6	106.4	107.3	55.2	51.6	76.5	92.5	75.9	130.7	90.1
1968–69	74.0	174.2	157.8	126.1	35.8	103.7	113.2	51.9	65.8	85.5	78.9	63.1	79.3	67.9
1969–70	61.1	144.5	108.0	114.8	80.6	116.7	132.8	58.1	117.8	108.2	103.4	90.7	92.1	90.9
1970–71	117.3	81.0	35.7	122.5	105.3	129.7	109.7	94.9	131.0	110.7	128.5	94.6	101.5	98.8

(Contd.)

Table 5–A : (Contd.)

	1	2	3	4	5	6	7	8	9		10	11	12	
1971–72	137.1	0.60	90.8	123.3	88.4	118.5	103.4	125.3	142.3	136.7	107.8	102.1	104.1	101.3
1972–73	37.0	74.3	187.4	71.4	130.3	117.9	101.9	161.7	115.5	126.8	98.9	109.1	67.6	99.4
1973–74	66.8	179.2	117.4	102.9	214.1	144.5	97.5	126.1	123.5	136.9	51.0	112.1	24.0	90.1
1974–75	103.3	139.6	108.1	83.0	149.8	170.6	91.2	117.3	267.8	151.4	20.5	158.2	31.7	124.0
1975–76	–276.0	78.4	40.0	64.9	25.6	77.2	98.7	128.9	219.7	79.2	87.3	129.9	22.6	113.5
1976–77	–3.0	126.4	102.8	91.0	21.8	119.3	125.0	144.8	95.3	86.9	194.2	140.7	49.4	135.6
1977–78	294.4	135.8	53.8	89.3	98.8	83.4	128.9	163.7	109.0	104.8	69.2	142.9	172.7	137.5
1978–79	375.3	106.3	–28.1	109.9	205.6	111.7	136.1	157.3	129.7	142.7	171.7	147.1	149.3	147.8
1979–80	295.7	131.0	34.2	107.8	222.3	102.6	127.6	168.8	155.1	155.1	136.8	129.6	154.1	132.1
1980–81	383.0	142.3	150.8	101.9	177.9	80.2	95.7	139.0	143.6	138.2	40.8	107.1	32.7	96.3
1981–82		107.3	138.9		122.7	58.3	88.9	156.7	96.1	113.6		99.9	90.4	104.4
1982–83		148.4	87.8		65.8	–0.1	102.7	109.2	79.9	81.8		82.5	264.0	109.6
1983–84		69.5	84.9		72.4	73.7	78.2	73.5	48.5	75.7		70.0	191.7	90.1
1984–85		54.8	106.1		57.6	84.2	86.4	55.1	73.8	74.1		94.1	189.9	97.6
1985–86		83.9	145.4		83.8	109.1	88.1	51.9	69.0	86.7		89.7	119.5	93.7
1986–87		63.8	131.9		72.8	90.7	74.0	48.2	51.8	77.6		59.4	72.2	61.8
1987–88		79.8	115.9		51.0	89.5	73.2	46.9	19.2	63.8		58.1	50.7	57.2
1988–89		76.5	107.1		73.3	152.0	86.6	60.8	41.6	70.8		85.4	5.7	74.5

Source : Table 3.1 and 3.2

Table 5–A : (Contd.)

Year	Transport Equipment	Electrical Machinery, apparatus & appliances	Machinery Other than Transport & Electrical Equipments	Ferrous/ Non-ferrous Metal Products	CAPITAL GOODS SECTOR	Jute Textiles	Other Chemical Products	Rubber & Rubber Products	INTERMEDIARY GOODS SECTOR	WHOLE MANUFACTURING SECTOR
	13	14	15	16		17	18	19		
1960–61	108.3	81.9	121.2	120.0	96.4	23.0	96.7	231.5	94.4	100.4
1961–62	120.1	84.4	56.2	26.1	98.9	–230.4	116.2	146.4	63.1	98.1
1962–63	124.3	105.7	103.2	93.3	110.2	44.6	101.4	144.4	172.8	97.4
1963–64	110.3	128.7	66.1	79.3	112.8	5.3	96.6	139.7	130.5	98.3
1964–65	120.8	127.9	81.2	51.6	122.8	116.0	114.5	136.1	77.2	101.5
1965–66	254.4	110.7	117.2	70.7	107.1	–363.0	119.2	126.5	98.2	93.5
1966–67	176.4	90.0	140.7	98.1	85.2	232.1	108.7	117.9	82.1	92.2
1967–68	71.2	76.2	54.2	48.8	65.4	–460.1	100.9	115.9	164.3	76.1
1968–69	59.2	48.7	68.4	116.9	53.9	–98.3	–51.7	110.0	102.9	73.4
1969–70	51.2	72.7	68.5	102.9	65.3	93.5	113.9	106.9	103.0	90.3
1970–71	76.3	91.4	127.7	102.5	100.7	714.6	113.9	102.1	103.1	102.9
1971–72	83.4	111.9	48.1	74.6	97.4	7552.4	106.9	99.5	133.1	104.6
1972–73	74.8	99.0	129.4	69.3	90.9	–4613.9	123.0	97.9	95.9	105.6

(Contd.)

Table 5–A : (Contd.)

	13	14	15	16		17	18	19		
1973–74	86.3	93.7	52.5	79.4	100.9	654.4	127.7	96.4	84.0	111.0
1974–75	87.7	116.8	56.1	72.1	116.7	1054.2	112.1	94.9	150.3	133.4
1975–76	84.2	103.0	91.1	29.7	97.7	284.8	104.7	91.1	9.0	87.4
1976–77	114.4	101.2	136.7	153.0	115.3	–313.9	134.2	91.2	–35.1	99.0
1977–78	106.4	110.0	72.4	66.7	111.4	130.6	127.2	88.0	92.4	113.9
1978–79	125.9	116.8	73.6	106.6	123.5	5.1	136.7	88.1	130.2	135.5
1979–80	125.6	145.2	+50.1	107.9	137.4	280.8	111.1	86.6	119.9	146.6
1980–81	143.8	165.7	158.1	127.4	149.9	68.8	128.4	82.8	142.9	133.3
1981–82	199.1	153.8	117.4	158.3	164.3	7.0	–49.9	80.2	147.5	137.4
1982–83	129.0	114.2	93.0	65.6	115.2	128.1	84.6	79.7	112.7	105.1
1983–84	96.6	83.5	142.0	75.7	88.2	423.4	128.8	79.2	84.5	85.4
1984–85	95.8	76.1	133.8	186.9	83.3	–170.2	95.8	61.6	65.8	82.4
1985–86	80.5	67.3	157.4	155.2	70.9	–3.4	106.7	61.6	76.3	80.6
1986–87	75.4	65.8	154.9	184.4	68.0	–32.8	92.3	58.4	91.3	70.4
1987–88	67.2	76.0	121.0	215.9	70.9	–52.7	106.2	43.4	88.6	66.3
1988–89	78.3	75.0	142.8	191.2	79.6	–30.7	94.5	32.3	122.4	79.3

Source : Table 3.2 and Appendix Table 5–A.

6

Profitability Trends and Business Cycles in U.K. Manufacturing

Significance of the Study of Profitability Trends and Business Cycles in U.K.

Industrialisation is a basic component of economic development and is the outcome of specialisation and generation of surpluses in each sector of the economy. Industrial activity plays an important role in providing employment opportunities, generating income, contributing to the maintenance and improvement of society's capital assets, and, in raising economic and social welfare. According to Jones and Cockerill (47, 1985) the relative importance of manufacturing sector in U.K. has declined and had been very slow, e.g., on average, the British economy grew at the rate of 2.5 per cent per annum since 1950. Moreover, the relative share of manufacturing sector declined from 36.7 per cent in 1950 and 1960 to 28.7 per cent to U.K.'s G.D.P. in 1978. This reflects that the absolute level of output of manufactured goods also declined over this period.

Jones and Cockerill (47, 1985) have observed that between 1970-79, U.K. lagged behind many other developed countries with respect to G.N.P. Growth which as recorded to be 1.6 per cent per annum for U.K., 2.7% for U.S.A., 3.7% for

Canada, 4.6% for Japan, 3.4% for France, 3.8% for Italy and 2.3% for West Germany. Slow growth of U.K. was accompanied by marked fluctuations in economic activity and around 4 to 5 year cycles were clearly identified. Peaks in 1964, 1973, etc., were observed to have coincided with general elections as incumbent government had boosted demand, especially for consumer goods, by reducing taxes and increasing the availability of money in the economy. Since these movements of economic activities cannot be predicted with accuracy, planing of business particularly of capital investment is found very difficult. These authors further argue that since 1974, the fluctuations in economic activity have occurred around much lower trend rate of growth than the years before it. Hence, it is predicted that the economy may fluctuate in the rest of the 1980s, but, may not show any significant overall expansion. This implied that U.K. may find it difficult to generate new employment opportunities which will make it difficult for her to reduce high level of unemployment which prevailed in 1980s.

Considering the views expressed above, it was felt that a closer look in the profitability ratios of British Manufacturing industries would enable us to throw further light on this sector as well as on the prevalance of business cycles in U.K. manufacturing. Following the methodology explained in Section II of Chapter 5 of the study, an attempt is made to detect deviation cycles in British manufacturing, alongwith the measurement of the periodicity and amplitude of these business cycles. Following conclusions are derived.

Detection of Deviation Cycles in British Manufacture

The figure of ratio of actual profit rate to trend value of profit rate for each U.K. manufacturing industries and sector over the period 1960-61 to 1988-89 are tabulated in Appendix Table 6–A. On the basis of close examination of this Table deviation cycles are detached. Following observations are made:

(A) Detection of Phases of Contraction and Expansion

Following points are noted from Table 6.1:

Table 6.1 : Periods of Contraction and Expansion in U.K. Manufacturing Sector : 1960–61 to 1988–89

Periods	Years						
Contraction	1960–63	1965–68	1970–72	1974–76	1979–81	1982–84	1986–87
Expansion	1963–65	1968–70	1972–74	1976–79	1981–82	1984–86	1987–89

Source : Appendix Table 6 (a)

(i) British manufacturing sector experienced period of contraction for seven times during 1960-61 to 1988-89, with the average period of contraction for the whole Manufacturing Sector being 2.5 years.

(ii) Similarly the period of expansion experienced by U.K. Manufacturing Sector during the study period also was for seven times, with the average period of expansion being 2.333 years.

(iii) Both the periods of contraction and expansion were dominated by 2 years period, though, sometimes the period was as short as 1 year or was extended upto 3 years also. These phases of contraction and expansion are determined on the basis of direction of the ratio of actual to trend value to profit rate and include majority of industries in the respective phase.

(iv) The number of industries undergoing the phases of contraction or expansion are presented in Table 6.2. The table shows that majority industries belonging to Consumer and Capital Goods Sectors, almost all belonging to Basic and Intermediary Goods Sector and most of the industries belonging to Whole Manufacturing Sector of U.K. underwent the periods of contraction as detected by the study.

(v) Similarly, most of the industries belonging to Whole Manufacturing Sector and Consumer Goods Sector, and almost all the industries belonging to Basic, Capital and Intermediary Goods Sectors, experienced the phases of expansion as denoted in Table 6.2. This confirms to the

Table 6.2 : Number of Industries in Contraction and Expansion Phase in the Ratio of Actual to Trend Value of Profit Rate in Indian Manufacturing Industries : 1960-61 to 1988-89

Total No. of Industries	Period of Contraction							SECTORS	Period of Expansion						
	1960–63	1965–68	1970–72	1974–76	1979–81	1982–84	1986–87		1963–65	1968–70	1972–74	1976–79	1981–82	1984–86	1987–89
9	9	9	7	9	8	5	4	CONSUMER GOODS SECTOR	8	9	9	9	8	6	7
2	2	2	2	2	2	2	1	BASIC GOODS SECTOR	2	2	2	2	1	2	2
5	5	4	5	5	4	3	4	CAPITAL GOODS SECTOR	5	5	5	5	4	4	4
1	1	1	1	1	0	1	1	INTERMEDIARY GOODS SECTOR	1	1	1	1	0	1	1
17	17	16	15	17	14	11	10	WHOLE MANUFACTURING SECTOR	16	17	17	17	13	13	14

Note : 1. Total number of industries in whole Manufacturing Sector is 17 and in Consumer Goods Sector is 9 upto 1976–77 and is 16 and 8 respectively from 1977–78 as data on Industry No. 8, i.e., Bricks, Pottery, Glass, Ceramics, etc., are not available from 1977–78.

observation made earlier by Jones and Cockerill [47,1985].

(vi) Above given observation, (No. iv and v) help us conclude strongly about the prevalence of the phases of contraction and expansion in U.K. manufacturing sector during 1960-61 to 1988-89.

(B) Periodicity of Business Cycles in U.K. Manufacturing

It was observed in Chapter V that business cycles were non-periodic in case of Indian Manufacturing Sector. This section intends to examine the periodicity of business cycles in U.K. manufacturing Sector. The method adopted is the same as in case of Indian manufacturing sector. Following points are noted from the results presented in Table 6.3, on periodicity of business cycles in U.K. manufacturing sector.

(i) Table 6.3 reveals that all industries belonging to Basic and Capital Goods Sector of U.K. Manufacturing Sector, underwent complete 5 or 6 Trough-Peak-Trough (TPT), or Peak-Trough-Peak (PTP) cycles during 1960-61 and 1988-89 alongwith majority of industries belonging to Consumer Goods Sector. However, a few industries belonging to Consumer Goods Sector and Intermediary Goods Sector (Other Manufacturing industries), experienced Complete 7 to 9 PTP/TPT cycles.

(ii) Bricks, Pottery, Glass, Ceramics, etc. which covered period of 17 years had smallest duration of complete 3 TPT/PTP cycles, while Tobacco and Clothing & Footwear had largest during of 8-9 TPT/PTP cycles.

(iii) Whole Manufacturing Sector, Basic and Capital Goods Sectors had complete 5 TPT/PTP cycles while Consumer Goods Sector experienced complete TPT and PTP cycles of 6 and 7 years respectively, while, Intermediary Goods Sector had complete 7 TPT/PTP cycles during the study period. Majority industries belonging to Consumer and Basic Goods Sectors and a few of capital goods Sector had complete TPT/PTP cycles above that of their respective sectors and Whole manufacturing Sector.

(iv) It may further be noted from Table 6.3 that majority of industries belonging to U.K.'s Consumer Goods Sector

Table 6.3 : Periodicity of Business Cycles in U.K. Manufacturing for the Ratio of Actual to Trend Value of Profit Rate

Industry	*Average No. of years of TPT cycles*	*No. of complete business cycles*	*Average no. of years of PTP cycles*	*No. of complete business cycles*
1. Food	3.50	6	3.33	6
2. Drink	3.71	7	3.83	6
3. Timber Furniture	3.67	6	4.00	6
4. Tobacco	3.00	8	3.00	9
5. Textiles	3.71	7	3.83	6
6. Clothing and Footwear	2.78	9	2.88	8
7. Leather, Leather Goods and Fur	3.71	7	3.50	6
8. Bricks, Pottery, Glass, Ceramics, etc.	2.33	3	4.00	3
9. Paper Printing and Publishing	4.17	6	4.80	5
CONSUMER GOODS SECTOR	3.83	6	3.86	7
10. Metal Manufacturing	4.17	6	4.60	5
11. Chemical & Allied Industries	3.83	6	4.00	6
BASIC GOODS SECTOR	4.60	5	4.80	5
12. Vehicles	4.80	5	4.80	5
13. Electrical Engineering Including Electronics	5.00	5	4.80	5
14. Non-Electrical Engineering	3.83	6	3.83	6
15. Metal Goods Not Elsewhere specified	4.00	5	4.80	5
16. Ship Building and Marine Engineering	4.33	6	3.80	5
CAPITAL GOODS SECTOR	5.00	5	4.80	5
17. Other Manufacturing Industries or Intermediary Goods Sector	3.43	7	3.43	7
WHOLE MANUFACTURING SECTOR	4.80	5	4.80	5

Note : * This industry covers the period 1960–61 to 1976–77, i.e., 17 years only.

and Intermediary Goods Sector had smaller average duration of both TPT and PTP cycles of below or around 3.71 for former and 4 years for latter. On the other hand side, majority ot industries belonging. On the other hand side, majority of industries belonging to Basic and Capital Goods Sector experienced the average duration of TPT/ PTP cycles around or above 4 years.

(vi) Table 6.3 further reveals that the average duration of TPT cycles for all the sector (except Capital Goods Sector) had below that of Whole manufacturing Sector (4.80 years). While for PTP cycles it was below or equal to Whole Manufacturing Sector.

It may therefore be concluded that U.K. manufacturing industries had complete 5 to 6 TPT/PTP cycles with average duration ranging between 2.78 to 5.00 years over the study period.

(C) Amplitude of Business Cycles in U.K. Manufacturing

Table 6.4 provides information on the amplitude of business cycles in U.K. Manufacturing, giving us the idea about the extent of rise and fall of profit rate during expansionary and contractionary phases of TPT/PTP cycles respectively during the period 1960-61 to 1988-89. The methodology adopted for estimation of the results of Table 6.4 is the same as presented earlier for Table 5.4 for Indian in Chapter V. Following observation are made.

(i) Columns 2 and 3 of Table 64 show that variation of actual profit from its trend value in case of rise ranged between 7.55% for Food to 664.75% for Ship Building and Marine Engineering, while with regards to fall, the variation was between 7.31% for Electrical Engineering including electronics to 539.38% for Ship Building and Marine Engineering over the study period.

(ii) As regards various sectors, columns 2 and 3 reveal that the Whole Manufacturing Sector of U.K. experienced a rise to the extent of 12.4% while Capital Goods Sector had 20.19% and a fall around 13.08% in former and 20.63%

Table 6.4 : Average Amplitude of Business Cycle and Average Amplitude per year of Series of Ratio of Actual to Trend Value of Profit Rate in U.K. Manufacturing Industries : 1960–61 to 1988–89

Industry	*Average Amplitude of Business Cycles (%)*		*Average Amplitudes per TPT Cycle (%age point)*		*Average Amplitude per Year for the (%age point)*	
	Rise	Fall	Rise	Fall	Rise	Fall
(1)	(2)	(3)	(4)	(5)	(6)	(7)
1. Food	7.55	10.25	16.07	15.15	14.96	10.45
2. Drink	12.41	8.70	16.97	18.14	8.81	11.43
3. Timber Furniture	29.67	24.04	50.80	49.82	32.65	29.65
4. Tobacco	11.20	15.36	19.87	19.84	13.28	16.27
5. Textiles	19.83	18.41	43.99	41.11	23.98	24.04
6. Clothing & Footwear	21.93	15.97	29.00	26.18	23.83	18.79
7. Leather, Leather Goods and Fur	29.71	36.46	56.86	49.17	23.64	37.64
8. Bricks, Pottery, Glass, Ceramics, etc.	11.89	10.63	24.10	25.43	9.55	21.53
9. Paper Printing & Publishing	13.36	21.17	33.08	32.83	14.54	16.14
CONSUMER GOODS SECTOR	8.36	10.15	19.01	38.26	10.28	10.80
10. Metal Manufacturing	27.92	39.63	69.32	53.13	43.56	22.97
11. Chemical and Allied Industries	14.43	16.68	30.23	29.95	16.20	15.25

(Contd.)

Table 6.4 : (Contd.)

Industry	*Average Amplitude of Business Cycles (%)*		*Average Amplitudes per TPT Cycle (%age point)*		*Average Amplitude per Year for the (%age point)*	
	Rise	Fall	Rise	Fall	Rise	Fall
(1)	(2)	(3)	(4)	(5)	(6)	(7)
BASIC GOODS SECTOR	14.76	20.63	35.83	35.14	13.65	17.24
12. Vehicles	75.71	96.08	236.13	204.80	56.57	115.93
13. Electrical Engineering Including Electronics	8.88	7.31	20.10	22.88	11.75	8.36
14. Non-Electrical Engineering	18.54	14.93	25.87	26.87	10.79	17.49
15. Metal Goods Not Elsewhere Specified	19.03	17.93	34.63	27.02	10.02	30.19
16. Ship Building and Marine Engineering	664.75	539.38	1722.10	1786.14	1594.77	965.37
CAPITAL GOODS SECTOR	20.19	18.61	50.13	50.94	21.54	16.48
17. Other Manufacturing Industries of INTERMEDIARY GOODS SECTOR	15.05	16.04	27.20	26.39	11.20	20.40
WHOLE MANUFACTURING SECTOR	12.40	13.08	28.45	28.60	11.67	10.68

Note : For details of estimates see the text.

in Basic Goods Sector. All other sectors except Consumers goods Sector, had larger extent of rise and fall.

(iii) These columns further reveal that except Food, all other industries belonging to Consumer goods Sector, except Chemical and Allied Industries of Basic Goods Sector, Electrical Engineering including electronics of Capital Goods Sector had rise above their respective sectoral rise. As regards fall, all industries belonging to respective sectors, except Drink of Consumer Goods Sector, Chemical and Allied Industries from Basic Goods Sector and Electrical Engineering including electronic belonging to Capital Goods Sector, had it above their respective sectors.

(iv) Columns 4 and 5 of Table 6.4 present average amplitude per TPT cycles for rise and fall respectively. It is observed that the average speed of rise ranged between 16.07 percentage points for Food to 1722.10 percentage points in case of Ship Building and Marine Engineering. As regards the average speed of fall it varied from 15.15 percentage points for former to 1786.14 percentage points for the latter industry during the study period.

(v) As regards the sectors, Consumers Goods Sector experienced smallest rise of 19.01 percentage points and Capital Goods Sector had the largest (50.13 percentage points). In case of fall, Intermediary Goods Sector experienced smallest (26.39 percentage points) fall while Capital Goods Sector had the largest fall (50.94 percentage points).

(vi) Except Consumer and Intermediary Goods Sectors in case of rise and the latter in case of fall, all other sectors had both rise and fall above that of Whole Manufacturing sector of U.K.

(v) Except Food, Drink, Tobacco, and Electrical Engineering including electronics all other industries experienced relatively high fluctuations in both the rise and fall.

(vi) The figures for average amplitude per year for the series for each U.K. manufacturing industry over the study period are presented in columns 6 and 7 of Table. 6.4. These estimates confirm the conclusions drawn above.

Drink with rise of 8.81 percentage profits in average amplitude per year, recorded the lowest while Ship Building and Marine Engineering had the largest rise of 159.77 percentage points. As regards fall, it was Food which had lowest average amplitude per year of 10.5 per centage points while Ship Building and Marine Engineering had the largest (965.37 percentage points).

(vii) The industries experiencing relatively less fluctuations in U.K. Manufacturing were Food, Drink, Tobacco, Bricks, Pottery, Glass, Ceramics, etc., Paper Printing and Publishing Chemical and Allied industries Electrical Engineering including Electronics Non-Electrical Engineering, Metal Goods not Elsewhere specified and Other Manufacturing industries in case of both rise and fall (i.e., 11 out of 17 industries).

(viii) Consumers goods sector had the lowest rise (10.28 percentage points) and fall (10.80 percentage points) in average amplitude per year while Capital Goods Sector had largest rise (21.54 percentage points) and Basic Goods Sector had largest fall (17.24) percentage points) during the study period.

Conclusion

The conclusions of the above given analysis can be summed up as follows:

(i) The British manufacturing sector underwent 7 phases of both the contraction and expansion during the period 1960-61 to 1988-89.

(ii) It was also observed that majority of industries had trough during contraction phase and peak during expansion phase.

(iii) Majority of U.K. Manufacturing industries experienced complete 5 to 6 TPT/PTP cycles while a few Consumer

Goods Industries and intermediary Goods Sector industry had complete 7 to 9 PTP/TPT cycles during the study period of 29 years.

(iv) The average duration of TPT/PTP cycle for majority of British manufacturing industries was below or around 4 years, while a few industries belonging to Basic and Capital Goods Sector had above 4 years.

(v) Majority of U.K. manufacturing industries experienced relatively smaller fluctuations over the study period. Metal Manufacturing, Vehicles and Ship Building and Marine Engineering industries experienced very wide fluctuations during this period.

APPENDIX TABLE 6–A : Actual Profit Rate as Percentage of Trend Value of Profit Rate for U.K Manufacturing Industries : 1960–61 to 1988–89

Year	Food	Drink	Timber furniture	Tobacco	Textiles	Clothing and Footwear	Leather, Leather Goods & Fur	Bricks, Pottery, Glass, Ceramics etc.	Paper Printing & Publishing	CONSUMER GOODS SECTOR	Metal Manufacturing	Cemicals & Allied Industries	BASIC GOODS SECTOR
	1	2	3	4	5	6	7	8	9		10	11	
1960–61	119.3	110.0	102.7	114.3	105.0	143.5	65.0	110.9	136.9	104.3	140.4	135.8	143.6
1961–62	112.0	101.4	80.6	120.5	95.0	126.9	62.8	108.8	121.5	112.7	109.9	103.8	109.8
1962–63	111.2	96.3	64.5	112.8	83.6	95.7	51.5	95.7	107.6	102.7	77.3	95.3	89.8
1963–64	110.5	97.6	49.9	112.4	98.8	90.2	91.7	97.9	104.2	104.9	74.2	101.2	92.0
1964–65	100.8	105.3	100.2	116.1	110.7	106.4	108.5	110.4	113.2	113.2	93.8	108.4	103.3
1965–66	99.5	98.1	88.5	112.3	108.6	91.1	93.4	100.9	105.9	104.8	93.4	98.8	101.0
1966–67	84.8	86.1	63.2	108.7	92.7	76.4	77.2	87.0	91.3	89.0	68.5	82.0	76.6
1967–68	87.0	83.9	47.2	78.9	91.5	85.6	60.4	89.8	83.3	87.0	95.6	83.2	85.9
1968–69	92.5	90.1	95.9	78.6	118.4	95.6	104.7	93.1	91.2	95.6	105.4	101.9	103.2
1969–70	83.6	89.3	78.6	88.8	106.5	93.5	122.9	81.6	82.8	89.5	116.7	99.0	101.9
1970–71	76.2	93.4	76.8	84.6	86.4	88.7	106.4	85.0	71.9	83.5	102.8	81.5	85.2
1971–72	79.7	102.3	126.8	91.4	97.2	113.5	137.9	106.5	69.8	91.1	96.0	79.8	82.1
1972–73	100.1	118.9	222.3	98.4	122.1	96.7	171.8	120.1	95.1	107.8	104.7	87.0	89.1

(Contd.)

Table 6–A : (Contd.)

	1	2	3	4	5	6	7	8	9		10	11	
1973–74	98.9	116.0	213.5	112.1	157.0	108.8	160.6	121.7	112.0	117.5	156.4	118.3	122.8
1974–75	97.8	93.7	130.5	62.9	131.2	79.9	123.3	80.3	108.7	95.4	131.4	151.7	147.1
1975–76	111.8	100.5	112.1	81.1	66.8	70.8	138.5	93.9	75.7	91.0	104.3	108.8	107.0
1976–77	134.4	114.9	137.1	91.1	109.6	70.9	168.2	115.8	100.4	113.2	132.7	120.5	120.9
1977–78	99.9	121.0	98.1	100.8	98.1	67.4	150.6		123.0	108.1	144.5	118.3	119.7
1978–79	105.2	124.4	111.2	97.0	99.1	154.8	107.3		141.7	112.9	121.8	101.7	102.2
1979–80	100.0	115.2	116.6	107.8	85.0	120.1	139.1		103.7	106.7	108.8	91.7	92.4
1980–81	84.7	84.1	44.3	85.8	21.5	96.8	29.7		51.6	68.3	27.4	40.1	38.1
1981–82	101.3	84.7	45.9	104.9	55.7	126.1	60.4		76.4	92.4	–7.6	76.0	66.4
1982–83	94.6	84.6	58.4	117.1	58.0	75.6	13.0		78.0	93.0	–21.0	71.3	66.6
1983–84	87.6	94.1	89.3	107.0	93.6	92.1	75.1		108.4	96.6	51.8	88.4	88.3
1984–85	100.9	97.5	86.6	119.3	127.4	61.5	102.9		104.0	105.8	121.6	104.9	107.1
1985–86	104.2	99.4	84.0	77.1	116.4	114.5	118.7		102.9	95.6	123.2	101.7	102.1
1986–87	102.1	91.1	101.3	102.8	113.7	116.0	113.6		117.5	101.3	76.0	103.7	103.4
1987–88	100.6	119.0	104.8	101.3	147.3	116.9	85.4		119.5	108.4	179.3	122.9	127.1
1988–89	106.4	88.1	106.6	120.1	103.7	115.6	60.4		105.7	111.1	171.3	127.2	129.1

Source : Table 4.2

(Contd.)

Table 5–A : (Contd.)

Year	Vehicles	Electrical Engineering including Electronics	Non-Electrical Engineering	Metal Goods Not Elsewhere specified	Ship Building and Marine Engineering	CAPITAL GOODS SECTOR	Other Manufacturing Industries (I.G.S.)	WHOLE MANUFACTURING SECTOR
	12	13	14	15	16		17	
1960–61	138.9	107.3	111.2	112.6	159.5	116.8	113.9	117.3
1961–62	85.4	91.2	104.0	93.3	142.3	94.2	103.3	104.9
1962–63	73.3	96.2	87.6	87.5	92.8	85.4	94.6	93.6
1963–64	115.5	101.0	86.9	89.1	96.0	95.5	104.4	98.7
1964–65	130.2	111.3	87.6	106.2	68.7	104.1	119.3	107.4
1965–66	127.5	97.6	93.2	98.5	–100.1	97.5	103.8	100.1
1966–67	103.1	92.2	87.5	90.0	21.1	90.2	92.6	86.5
1967–68	79.0	90.5	83.9	91.1	161.4	85.8	92.8	87.0
1968–69	120.1	104.0	86.8	95.4	284.6	99.4	108.7	99.0
1969–70	120.5	87.9	101.0	104.2	–484.8	97.8	100.6	95.1
1970–71	29.5	85.8	91.0	108.7	–39.7	87.0	97.2	85.5
1971–72	106.0	85.6	92.4	107.5	–510.0	95.5	96.0	91.6
1972–73	114.4	107.6	104.4	110.3	1871.7	113.3	99.7	105.9
1973–74	147.6	113.3	120.0	124.4	–5601.7	123.3	102.6	120.5

(Contd.)

Table 6–A : (Contd.)

	12	13	14	15	16		17	
1974–75	51.6	100.5	121.4	147.7	−7594.0	118.1	97.2	113.2
1975–76	−55.1	99.5	115.7	110.1	323.4	101.6	98.8	97.9
1976–77	62.6	124.2	137.6	119.3	−507.8	140.8	125.7	123.5
1977–78	299.3	119.5	166.0	93.5	−626.7	152.1	122.2	124.9
1978–79	230.2	105.5	133.3	94.2	−100.3	121.3	85.6	112.6
1979–80	153.9	101.9	117.0	103.5	−3.6	117.6	86.5	106.3
1980–81	−164.0	88.8	88.6	77.2	87.7	69.8	65.7	65.1
1981–82	−100.7	93.6	90.0	58.2	152.0	−15.6	66.9	52.4
1982–83	−38.0	99.6	53.8	49.2	703.4	68.9	35.6	77.6
1983–84	35.0	106.3	67.3	52.3	109.8	88.0	67.3	91.1
1984–85	160.0	111.0	87.1	73.5	104.9	116.0	103.1	109.3
1985–86	204.3	97.5	102.6	88.1	95.8	113.3	157.0	104.0
1986–87	−11.5	85.0	80.0	107.3	92.9	81.4	109.3	95.8
1987–88	249.34	94.6	97.6	144.4	81.7	114.6	125.3	114.7
1988–89	466.1	97.4	106.8	160.2	58.4	131.5	127.5	121.3

Source : Table 4.2 and 4.3.

7
A Comparative Analysis : Conclusions

The Significance of Comparative Study

The initiation of the process of privatization by Thatcher Government in early 1980's in U.K. brought about a global transformation with a breath taking speed and breadth. It embraced more than 50 countries of the world with varied political, social and economic ideologies. The period of early 1990s witnessed the break-up of erstwhile U.S.S.R., and Union of East and West Germany. In short, the wave of privatization mesmerised the entire world.

The author had discussed in her article (Rede, 80, 1987) about various forces that have led various countries to adopt the policy of privatisation. The most important amongst these are importance of increase in competition, efficiency, productivity and growth of a concern, application of theory of comparative costs, for economic pragmatism so that political commitments in favour of free competition could be kept, for technological and financial gains, for correcting dismal financial performance of State Owned Enterprises, and for correcting country's financial imbalances, etc. The major thrust of these factors in an opening up of industries for both, the domestic and international markets, via encouragement of free competition which would enhance efficiency, productivity and growth of a concern, the industry and the economy, through technology upgradation. This has reinforced the people's belief in efficient working of price-profit mechanism.

As stated earlier, the wave of privatisation has enveloped all types of economic systems, e.g., developed capitalist countries like U.S.A., U.K., France, Japan, etc., alongwith developed communist countries, like erstwhile U.S.S.R., Hungary, Yugoslavia, etc., and also developing mixed economies like India, Bangladesh, Singapore, Malaysia, etc. The global chain of events since early 1980s has induced us to probe into the financial performance of manufacturing sectors of two different economies, viz., India, a developing mixed economy and U.K., a developed capitalist economy.

It has been widely accepted by economists, that, under perfect competition, the rate of return on investment tends to fall in the long run for any industry, due to competition among the entrepreneurs, factor substitution, etc. Entrepreneurs, under perfect competition would like to leave relatively unprofitable industries and enter the profitable ones. Profitability is a yardstick that measures the financial performance of any concern and plays pivotal role in the growth process of concern, the industry, and the economy. The movement of capital from non-profitable to profitable fields, is crucial to the efficiency and growth of the economy and is explained by factors like free entry and exist of firms in industry, price-profit mechanism. the principle of factor substitution, etc.

Adoption of the policy of privatisation in one or the other form (Rede, 82, 1989) implies encouraging competition within the country and opening up for the world market, leading to marketisation of economic activities in those economic which have adopted it. As stated earlier, the cyclical fluctuations are found to be an ever present force in market economies based on free enterprise system.

Thus, the chain of events since early 1980s has evoked us to probe into an enquiry of profitability trends and business cycles of two countries with different political, social and economic ideologies, viz., India and U.K. Before we begin with the comparative analysis a word on economic background of these two economies would not be out of the place here.

Mixed Economy: India, Viz-A-Viz, Capital Economy

(A) Indian Economy

India is a glaring example of Mixed Economy. It encompasses co-existence of great variety of forms of organizations and techniques of production in the operation. India also provides an example of amazing medley of restrictions and regulations, of undirected and uncontrolled private sector of the economy.

With the adoption of the philosophy of "Socialistic Pattern of Society", Industrial policy packages framed since independence were governed by these principles and directions whereby social gain, and not private profits would be the determinant of planned economic development of the country. Industrial Policy Resolutions (IPR) of 1948 and 1956 provided the basic frame for industrial policies in India and the latter IPR was considered to be the Economic Constitution", of the country. The State was assigned progressively dominant role in speedy industrialisation of the country. IPR 1956 assigned 17 industries of the State as the exclusive monopoly of the State (Industries belonging to Schedule A attached to industries Act, 1951), while 12 industries belonging to basic and strategic areas (Schedule B) were to be progressively State owned. The remaining industries were left to private sector, but were to be regulated and guided by the State. In short, industries belonging to basic and strategic importance, requiring heavy investment and with nature of public utility services were to remain under the control of public sector.

The period from 1948 to 1985, especially from 1956 to 1975 witnessed increasing State control and regulations in India. The philosophy of socialistic pattern of society embedded in IPR 1956, the establishment of planning Commission implicit in IPR 1948, conferred on Indian Government, the power of regulating production and expansion of industries, while deliberately speeding up industrial process via widening state activity in the Industrial Sector. The adverse effect of excessive controls in Indian industry is revealed through decline in annual compound growth rate of Index Numbers of Industrial Production from 9% in 1960-65 to -1.6% in 1979-80.

Country experienced very slow industrial growth (around 4% to 5% per year) till mid-seventies due to defective implementation of policies. These policies gave rise to growth of corruption, bribery, lack of work culture, inertia and sloth. The need for relieving the economy from long persistent and widely stretched economic controls was expressed by various committees and u-turn in economic thought and events took place. Though halty and slow, a move in the direction of greater economic freedom and marketisation was made via recommendations of various committees adopted to look into the issues faced by India Industries since mid–1970s. This process of "liberalisation" or "opening up" got tremendous momentum from 1985 and was ascentuated further by New Economic Policy and New Industrial Policy of June 1991. It may, however be noted, that in case of India share of registered Manufacturing in real NDP increased from 6,9% in 1960–61 to 8.5% in 1975–76 (see Misra & Puri, 61, 1991).

In view of this background for Indian manufactuing sector, it was felt that an examination of profitability trends for Indian manufacturing industries between the period 1960–61 to 1988–89 would throw very interesting results. Majority of this period, viz., 1960 to 1985 can be considered to be a period of controls, regulations, etc., especially the period 1960–75 because of which expansion of industries and industrial growth could have been adversely affected. Controls on prices, distribution, investment, etc., would also have affected the profitability of these industries adversely.

Though one may also expect that this was the period of speedy industrialisation in the country, and hence, the industries would have not only growth fast, but reaped increasing returns over their investments. This would have been the situation, had the manufacturing private sector industries enjoyed free competition and no controls. Hence, a tendency of declining profitability is expected to have prevailed in this period. The conclusions of Chapter 3 of the study confirm this.

Moreover, the industries covered here belong to private

corporate sector, and hence, it is expected that their earning would have been liable to business cycles. This was examined in Chapter 5 of this study.

A similar type of analysis is undertaken for British Manufacturing Industries. Before we make a comparative analysis of the results drawn earlier, few words on description of U.K. economy especially manufacturing sector of U.K. is given below:

(B) British Economy

U.K. had been the leader of the process of industrialisation in 18th century and privatisation since early 1980s. Privatisation was the outcome of the general recognisation that British Manufacturing industry had performed poorly in comparison with its foreign competitors since last 4-5 decades. Since industrial activity contributes to economic development, and, at the same, time, is also the product of that process of development, its poor performance over half of this century was a cause of concern for politicians economists, academicians, etc. U.K. being one of the highly developed capitalist economy, industries in manufacturing sector enjoyed free competition, advanced techniques of production and required skills and experienced personnel to operate complex equipment. Inspite of this, U.K. experienced a fall in the relative importance of industrial sector, especially a decline of manufacturing sector from 1950.

As mentioned in Chapter VI, not only had the relative share of manufacturing in U.K.'s GNP declined since 1950 (36.7%) till 1978 (28.7%) the absolute level of output of this sector has also fallen over this period. This process of fall in relative importance of the manufacturing sector, as measured by output, employment, or capital investment, has been termed, "de-industrialisation." This is a cause of concern, because, future employment opportunities and nation's capacity to raise living standards of its citizens would adversely be affected by this process. Though share of manufacturing industry in total output is expected to fall as an advance industrialized economy develops further, this occurs due to increased investment in heavy industries, communication systems, etc. Similar, with further development, people spend additional income on output of the services sector and since these activities are typically labour intensive, it is not necessarily a cause of concern.

For a country like U.K., with its population around 60 million in early 1980s and with more than one-third of total national income derived from foreign trade, it is risky to concentrate increasingly on the output of services, as it is manufacturing industries that provide the bulk of employment in U.K. Since the manufactured products of U.K. are traded widely on the world markets, it is necessary to have a viable, profitable and competitive manufacturing sector so that the country can achieve sustained economic growth and continued employment opportunities.

It is claimed that two main factors have been responsible for the process of de-industrialisation in U.K. "Crowding out" of output and investment in the marketed sector of the economy by increased resource absorption in the non-marketed sector (especially the public sector) had been one factor while progressive loss of international competitiveness had been the other. The former has not been proven, chiefly because, high level of unemployment prevailed in case of both labour and capital in U.K. Poor internatonal competitiveness is attributed to a number of factors like overvalued exchange rate, low productivity, and non-price factors of quality, design, delivery and after-sales service.

In order to enhance growth, productivity and profitability of manufacturing industries, U.K. adopted various policies to promote competition, e.g., with mergers, dominant firms and restrictive practices (see Jones and Cockerill, 47, 1984). There have been changes in investment aid in the sixties from tax allowance to cash grants and back again to tax allowances. Though the policies regarding price-control, role of National Economic Development Council (NEDC), planning, use of subsidies etc. have been, to some extent, continuous, these have changed direction with each change in government, causing disruption in industrial development of U.K. This situation induced Thatcher government in U.K. to favour privatisation on practical grounds. U.K.'s political commitments in favour of free competition led to its wide recognition and acceptance, not only in U.K., but all over the world.

Growth of Economy and Industry In India and U.K.

Before taking up the comparison of results on profitability trends and business cycles in U.K. and India, little information about the rate of growth of national income and industrial sector, especially manufacturing sector will be highly useful.

India is a developing mixed economy and aims at attaining planned economic development via speedy industrialisation. Major activities of her manufacturing sector, e.g., prices, production, expansion, investment, distribution, etc., are regulated and directed by the State and some of these are directly under State sector. Obviously, the prevalence of free competition in manufacturing sector is essentially lacking.

On the other hand, U.K. is highly developed and industrialised capitalist economy with relatively more competitive manufacturing sector. with no State regulations. Hence, it is expected that industries under less competitive and regulated Indian manufacturing sector would be less profitable than those operating under free U.K. industrial sector. Following statistics provide us information regarding the growth of these two countries and their industrial sectors.

(i) The annual rate of growth of GNP (Gross National Product) for the period 1965-1988 was estimated to be 1.8% for both U.K. and India. However, G.N.P. per capita in U.S. dollars in 1988 was estimated to be 12810 for U.K. and 340 for India. i.e., U.K. enjoyed GNP per capita about 37.7 times greater than India in 1988, though both had the same growth rates of GNP. This is a clear reflection of very high level of standard of living attained by U.K. in comparison with India. It may, however be noted that amongst the underdeveloped regions, India claimed second lowest GNP (China had lowest) per capita in U.S. dollars in 1988 while U.K. ranked second lowest (Spain had lowest) amongst developed regions (see Misra and Puri, 61, 1991, pp. 15 and 25). These authors have further shown that U.K. also had lowest average annual rate of growth of GNP (1.8%) between 1965-88 as compared to other developed countries, e.g., Japan (4.3%), West Germany (2.5%), France, (2.5%), and Italy (3.0%). Thus, U.K. ranked lowest, amongst selected developed countries in terms of both, GNP growth rate and GNP per capita in U.S. dollars.

(ii) As regards the contribution of industrial (Secondary) Sector in real G.D.P. (Gross Domestic Product) for India, it rose from 18.7% in 1960-61 to 22.3% 1970-71 and 24.3% in 1980-81 and 26.9% in 1988-89 (See Misra and Puri, 61, 1991, p.74). For U.K., contribution of industry in real GDP was estimated to be around 48.3% in 1960-61, and declined to 44.4% in 1970-71 and 41.2% in 1978 (See Jones and Cockerill, 47, 1985, p.6). Similarly, share of registered manufacturing in India's real NDP increased from 6.9% in 1960-61 to 8.3% in 1970 and 8.5% in 1975 (See Misra and Puri, 61, 1991, p. 257). U.K.'s manufacturing sector claimed its share in real GDP around 36.7% in 1960-61, 32.7% in 1970-71 and 28.7% in 1978.

A close examination of above statistics indicates very high level and significance of industrial sector in U.K. the proportion of which in GDP remained above 2.5 times that of India in 1960–61, double in 1970–71, and slightly below it by end of 1970's. Or, in other words, U.K.'s industrial sector commanded almost half of GDP in 1960 while for India the share was around one-fifth. Though, share of industry in U.K. had continuous decline over the period 1960–79, and India enjoyed a rise, the former still continued to have lion's share of industrial sector in GDP (40% in 1978) as compared to India (24% in 1980–81). We observe the similar tendencies in case of manufacturing sector the share of which has though grown in case of India between 1960–75, and that for U.K. declined, the latter continued to command much higher contribution to national income than the former.

Profitability Trends: Comparison of Manufacturing Sectors of India and U.K.

It is essential to point out here that the concepts and

methodology used in this study are comparable and cover the same period: 1960-61 to 1988-89. An attempt has been made to adjust the concept of profit rate for Indian manufacturing industries in accordance with that adopted for U.K. Moreover, the data relied upon for both countries relates to the consolidated accounts for joints stock, listed companies, classified according to industrial classification as per their main activities. The profit rate concept used for the study is a financial concept and is chosen considering its popular use and easiness in its calculation. It faces a number of limitations as mentioned in Chapter I. Following conclusions are derived from the examination of profitability trends in Indian and British manufacturing industries.

(i) Majority of Indian manufacturing industries, 15 out of 19 (78.9%), suffered a lower profit rate in 1988-89 as compared to 1960-61, while only four industries, viz., Sugar, Tobacco, Other Chemical Products and Rubber & Rubber Products had higher profit rate in 1988-89 as compare to 1960-61.

However, as regards U.K. manufacturing industries, majority of these, 10 out of 17 (58.8%) enjoyed a higher profit rate in 1988-89 than in 1960-61, while seven industries suffered a fall. Majority of capital goods industries (except Electrical Engineering including electronics) and 3 consumer goods industries suffered a set back to their earning power. Thus, the profitability trend results for manufacturing industries of India are quite opposite to those derived for U.K.

(ii) As regards the variations in decline, Pottery,. China, etc., industry experienced lowest fall of 0.8 percentage points while Jute had largest fall of 27.2 percentage points in these years. The extent of rise enjoyed by U.K. manufacturing industries varied from 0.5 percentage points for Leather, Leather Goods and Fur to 11.4 percentage points for Tobacco during these years. Thus, variation in decline for Indian manufacturing industries had been much wide than in case of rise for U.K. manufacturing industries.

(iii) The variation in percentage point rise for profit rate of Indian industries was recorded to be between 2 for Sugar and 5.4 for other Chemical Industries, while, variation in decline of profitability of U.K. industries stood around 0.5 percentage points for Non-Electrical Engineering and 15.2 percentage points for Ship Building and Marine Engineering in 1988 over 1960-61. Here, the Indian industries had smaller variation in rise, while, British Industries has relatively larger variation in fall of profit rate over the study period.

(iv) As regards sectors, all the sectors of Indian manufacturing, except Intermediary Goods Sector, had fall in profit rate while all the sectors of U.K. manufacturing had rise in profitability in 1988-89 as compared to 1960-61. During this period, India's capital goods sector had smallest decline of 6.7 percentage point and Consumer Goods Sector had largest fall of 16.5 percentage points. As regards U.K., Capital Goods Sector had smallest rise of 2.5 percentage points while Basic Goods Sector had largest rise of 8.1 percentage points. In short, though almost all the sectors are experiencing the same tendency in profit rate, the magnitude of sectoral decline in profit rates for Indian manufacturing in observed to be much larger than that of sectoral rise in case of U.K. manufacturing.

(v) The above given results, based on the first and the last year of the study are further confirmed by Time Trend analysis of profitability.

It has been observed in Chapter 3 and 4 that Time trend Results of Linear Bivariate Model for profitability of Indian manufacturing industries are statistically significant in case of 8 out of 19 industries (42.1%) and 9 out of 17 industries (52.9%) for U.K. respectively. These results further confirm that profitability had a strong tendency to decline in case of all the 8 Indian manufacturing industries while 6 U.K. manufacturing industries had a rising trend in profit rate while 3 had a declining tendency.

R^2, the Coefficient of determination has been found to be statistically significant in case of all these industries and confirms the goodness of fit. The value of R^2 varied from 0.154 for Electrical Machinery, Apparatus and Appliances to 0.633 for Silk-Rayon and Woollen Textiles as regards Indian Manufacturing. For U.K., R^2 for industries with declining profit rate varied between 0.154 for Vehicles and 0.206 for Metal Goods Not Elsewhere Specified. the value of R^2 for those U.K. manufacturing industries for which profitability had a rising trend, varied between 0.147 for Other Manufacturing Industries to 0.767 for Electrical Engineering including electronics.

These results imply that time explains profitability trends in different degrees in these two countries.

(vi) The declining tendency of 8 Indian and 3 U.K. manufacturing industries is revealed by the negative sign and statistically significant values of β, the time trend Coefficient. β assumed the values between –0.298 for Electrical Machinery, Apparatus and Appliances and –1.179 for Grains and Pulses for India, while its values for U.K. varied between –0.203 for Metal Goods Not Elsewhere Specified and –0.507 for Ship Building and Marine Engineering, indicating larger variations in decline of Indian industries as compared to U.K. industries.

The variations in rising trend of U.K. manufacturing industries were small for value of β and ranged between 0.178 for Other Manufacturing Industries to 0.385 for Electrical Engineering including electronics.

As regards trends in profitability of Sectors, β varied from -0.172 for Whole Manufacturing Sector to -0.278 for Consumer Goods Sector for Indian manufacturing, While β assumed values around 0.153 for Whole Manufacturing Sector and 0.268 for Basic Goods Sector of U.K. manufacturing Sector. The sectoral variations in both, fall for Indian and rise for U.K. manufacturing, seem to be quite small.

(vii) The industries experiencing decline in their earning power in India are Grains and Pulses, Silk-Rayon and Woollen Textile, Medicines and Pharmaceutical Preparations (3 out of 9 industries of Consumer Goods Sector), Cement (1 out of 4 industries belonging to Basic Goods Sector) Electrical Machinery, Apparatus and Appliances; Ferrous/Non-Ferrous Metal Products (2 out of 4 industries from Capital Goods Sector) and Jute, Textiles (1 out of 3 Intermediary Goods Sector Industries). It is obvious here that these industries cover all the sectors, and thus, it implies that differences in the nature of industry, their age-structure, and uses etc., exerted no influence on profitability trends of these industries in India, because, all these industries suffered a set back to their earnings capacity, irrespective of the sector to which these belonged over the study period 1960-61 to 1988-89.

As regards U.K., only three industries suffered a set back to their profitability, viz., Vehicles, Metal Goods Not Elsewhere Specified and Ship Building and Marine Engineering. All these industries belong to Capital Goods Sectors.

The six industries which enjoyed rising trend in profitability incase of U.K. manufacturing sectors are, Food, Tobacco, Paper Printing and Publishing (3 out of 9 industries from Consumer Goods Sector), Chemical and Allied Industries (1 out of 2 Basic Goods Industries), Electrical Engineering including electronics (1 out of 5 capital Goods Industries) and, Other Manufacturing Industries or Intermediary Goods Sector. Thus, it is obvious here that irrespective of their nature and sectors, industries have experienced rising tendency in their earning rate in U.K. also over the study period.

From the above given analysis of Profitability trends for Indian and U.K. manufacturing industries for the period of 29 years, i.e., 1960-61 to 1988-89, it is further observed that as regards India, a few Consumer, Basic and Intermediary Goods Industries alongwith majority industries belonging to Capital Goods Sectors, experienced declining profit rate. Similarly, in U.K., majority of Capital Goods Industries were hard hit from falling tendency in their profitability. This implies that during the study period, the Profitability of majority of Basic and

Capital Goods industries was adversely affected in these two countries.

Dispersions in Rates of Profit: Comparison of Indian and U.K. Manufacturing Sectors

Dispersions in rates of profit of industries are revealed through the mean value of the series for each industry over the study period, and, values of coefficient of variations for these industries.

(i) It is observed in Chapter 3 that, in India, medicines and Pharmaceutical Industry had the highest mean rate of Profit (31.0%) while Jute Textiles had negative and the lowest (-3.6%) during the study period of 29 years. In case of U.K., Tobacco enjoyed highest mean profit rate (17.8%) and Ship Building and Marine Engineering had negative and lowest rate of profit (–0.3%) over this period. Thus, in both the countries, highest profitability was enjoyed by an industry belonging to Consumer Goods Sector while lowest was experienced by an industry belonging to Intermediary Goods Sector for India, and Capital Goods Sector for U.K.

It may further be observed from these figures that the highest mean rates of Profit enjoyed by Indian industry was 1.74 times higher than experienced by U.K. industry. Similarly, the lowest mean profit rate experienced by Jute industry of India is 12 times lower than that experienced by Jute industry of India is 12 times lower than that experienced by Ship Building and Marine Industry of U.K. In other words, Indian manufacturing industries experienced larger variations in their mean rates of profit than did the U.K. manufacturing industries.

(ii) As regards India, 11 out of 19 (57.9%) manufacturing industries belonging to Consumer, Capital and Intermediary Goods Sector enjoyed higher mean rate of profit than experienced by Whole Manufacturing Sector (mean profit rate = 16.4%). Amongst the Sectors, Capital Goods

Sector had highest mean profit rate of 19.2% as against lowest 15.0% experienced by Basic Goods Sector.

In case of U.K., 9 out of 17 (52.9%) manufacturing industries, most of which belonged to Consumer and Basic Goods Sector, had higher mean rate of profit than the Whole Manufacturing Sector (14.8%). Amongst the sectors, Consumers, Goods Sector enjoyed highest mean rate of 15.5% and Capital Goods Sector suffered from lowest mean rate of profit of 14.0% over the study period.

These statistics reveal that not only majority of industries experienced higher mean rate of profit than Whole Manufacturing Sector in both India and U.K., but most of these belonged to Consumer Goods Sector.

(iii) Another interesting observation made is that mean rate of profit for Indian manufacturing industries varied greatly irrespective of the sectors to which these belong. However, in case of U.K. the Consumer Goods industries had less variations in mean profit rate compared to Basic and Capital Goods industries.

(iv) The relative dispersion in the series for profit rate is captured by the value of coefficient of variations (C.V.) It is observed that in case of India, Tobacco had smallest dispersions in the series of profit rate (C.V.=0.185) while Jute Textiles had largest dispersions (C.V. =-7.548) during the period 1960-61 to 1988-89. As regards U.K., Drink industry had lowest variations (C.V.=0.123) While Ship Building and Marine Engineering had the highest (C.V.=-35.49%) over this period.

Thus, in both the countries, lowest variations in the profitability series are experienced by Consumer Good industries while highest were experienced by industry belong to Intermediary Goods Sector in India, and, Capital Goods Sector in U.K.

In India, Whole Manufacturing Sector, while in U.K., Consumers Goods Sector enjoyed smallest variations as C.V. was 0.215 for former and 0.153 for latter.

Intermediary Goods Sector of India had widest fluctuations in profitability (C.V.=0.448), and, Capital Goods Sector of U.K. had largest variations (C.V.).292) over the study period.

(vi) In case of India, 13 out of 19 industries, i.e., 68.4%, experienced moderately fluctuating variations inthe Profit rate series as C.V. ranged between 0.250 to 0.500 for these industries. As regards U.K., 7 out of 17 industries (41.2%) had relatively stable variations as C.V. has been observed to be below 0.250, and 8 industries (47.1%) experienced moderate fluctuations (C.V. was between 0.250 and 0.500). In short, as against 68.4% Indian industries enjoying moderate fluctuations in profitability during the study period, about 88.2% British industries experienced moderate or less than moderate, i.e., relatively stable, fluctuations in their profit rate series.

Only Tobacco had relatively stable fluctuations in profitability as regards Indian manufacturing sector, while 3 industries, viz., Cotton Textiles, Paper and Paper Products and Cement had highly fluctuating profitability series (C.V. between 0.501 to 0.750). As regards U.K., two industries belonging to Capital Goods Sector, viz., Vehicles and Ship Building and Marine Engineering had erractically fluctuating variations (C.V was above 0.751) while Grains and Pulses and Jute Textiles experienced the erratic fluctuations in profitability series of Indian manufacturing during the study period.

In sum, fluctuations in profit rate series of Indian manufacturing industries were wider than experienced by U.K. manufacturing industries, and the latter exhibited relatively stable series, though with relatively smaller mean rate of profit over the study period.

Profitability Trends and Business Cycles in India and U.K.

Chapters 5 and 6 have explored the existence of business cycles on the basis of profitability trends for manufacturing sectors of India and U.K. respectively over the period 1960-61 to 1988-89. Following observations are made.

(A) Phases of Business Cycles

It is interesting to observe that manufacturing sectors of India and U.K. have been influenced by the economic fluctuations, as is indicated by the analysis of the ratio of actual to trend rate of profit for each industry over the study period.

(i) For both, India and U.K., period of contraction is detected for 7 times, and, period of expansion, too, is found to prevail for 7 times. The average period of contraction being 2.8 years for Indian manufacturing and 2.5 years for British manufacturing. Similarly average period of expansion is observed to be of 3 years for former and 2.333 years for the latter country. In other words, the duration of average period for contraction and expansion for Indian manufacturing has been slightly greater than it is for U.K. manufacturing sector over the study period of 29 years.

(ii) Both the contractionary and expansionary periods in India varied between 1 to 3 years, the former being dominated by 2 years' period and the latter by 3 years' period. As against this, these phases were dominated by 2 years' period for U.K., though some variation between 1 to 3 years also existed. Obviously, except for few years, these phases do not exactly coincide for the two countries.

(iii) Majority of Indian manufacturing industries experienced these phase of contraction and expansion during the periods detected.Same is true for U.K. manufacturing industries. Moreover, majority industries had trough during contractionary phase and, peak during expansionary phase, as regards both the countries.

(B) Periodicity of Business Cycle

A business cycle is said to be complete when it moves from Trough to Peak and to next trough (TPT cycles), or movement of Peak-Trough-Peak (PTP cycle). Following results are derived:

(i) In case of India and U.K., both, majority of industries belonging to consumer and Basic Goods Sector (all industries for U.K. and also of Capital Goods Sector) experienced complete 5 to 6 TPT/PTP cycles during the study period. However, majority industries belonging to Capital and Intermediary goods sectors of Indian manufacturing, had complete 8 to 9 TPT/PTP cycles, while, a few British Consumer Goods and Intermediary Goods industry had complete 7 to 9 TPT/PTP cycle during the study period.

(ii) Rubber and Rubber Products industry had minimum complete 2 TPT nd 1 PTP cycle for India, while Bricks, Ceramics, Glass etc., had minimum 3 TPT/PTP cycles for U.K. manufacturing.

(iii) Maximum complete 9 TPT/PTP cycles in India were experienced by Machinery (Other than Transport Equipment), Jute Textiles and Other Chemical Products, whereas in U.K. Tobacco experienced complete 8 TPT/PTO cycles while Clothing and Footwear had complete 9 TPT/PTP cycles.

In other words majority of Indian and British manufacturing industries, belonging to all sectors, had complete 5-6 TPT/PTP cycles. However, majority of Capital and Intermediary industries of India, and a few Consumer and Intermediary industries of U.K. had longer, complete 8-9 TPT/PTP cycles, indicating that these are more prone to economic fluctuations than others.

(iv) As regards sectors, While Manufacturing and Capital Goods Sectors, both had complete 4-5 TPT/PTP cycles in case of both India and U.K. (alongwith Basic Goods Sector for U.K.), While Consumer Goods Sector had complete 6 TPT/PTP cycles in both countries. Basic and Intermediary goods sector of India had complete 8-9 TPT/PTP cycles while Intermediary goods sector of U.K. had complete 7 TPT/PTP cycles during the study years.

(v) Majority of industries in both the countries experienced larger complete TPT/PTP cycles than their respective sectors.

(vi) The average duration of complete TPT cycles for India ranged between 2.71 years for Tobacco to 6.50 years for Rubber & Rubber Products, while in case of U.K. it varied between 2.78 years for Clothing and Footwear to 5 years for Electrical Engineering including Electronic. Thus, the variation is observed to be longer for Indian manufacturing than British manufacturing as regards the Average duration of TPT cycle. The average period for PTP cycle varies from 2 years for Rubber and Rubber Products to 6.25 years for Electrical Machinery, Apparatus and Appliances for India, while for U.K. it ranges between 2.88 years for Clothing and Footwear to 4.8 years for Paper Printing and Publishing, Vehicles, Electrical Engineering including Electronics and Metal Goods not Elsewhere Specified. The earlier observation holds for this also.

(vii) Majority of Indian manufacturing industries experienced average duration of TPT/PTP cycles below or around 4.33 years, while majority of U.K.'s Consumer Goods and Intermediary Goods industries had it below or around 3.71 (TPT) or 4 (PTP) years.

(C) Amplitude of Business Cycles

This section of the study examined the extent of variation of actual profit rate from its trend value for each industry over 29 years period. following conclusions are derived for India and U.K.

(i) As regards India, Tobacco had lowest rise of 14.88 per cent in case of variation of actual profit rate from its trend value, while Jute Textile had the highest rise of 260.47%. The similar figures for U.K. are 7.55% for Food and 664.75% for Ship Building and Marine Engineering in this period.

Variation of actual profit rate from its trend value in case of fall was accounted to be lowest, 15.06, for India's Medicines and Pharmaceutical Preparations and highest,

248.84% for Jute Textiles. In case of U.K. Electrical Engineering including electronics recorded lowest variation of 7.31% while Ship Building and Marine Engineering had largest fall of 539.38%.

(ii) Whole Manufacturing Sector in both the countries recorded lowest rise and fall, as regards the variation of actual profit rate from its trend value. Intermediary goods Sector for India recorded highest rist and fall while, Capital Goods Sector of U.K. experienced highest rise, while Basic Goods Sector had highest fall in amplitude of business cycles.

(iii) It is observed, that, most of agro-based industries, viz., Grains and Pulses, Edible Vegetable and Hydrogenated Oils, Sugar, Cotton Textiles, Silk-Rayon and Woolen Textiles, Paper and Paper Products and Jute Textiles as well as those belonging to Basic, Capital and Intermediary Goods Sector had both rise and fall above that of their respective sectors, and also above the whole Manufacturing Sector, Similar tendency is observed in case of most of the industries of U.K.

(iv) Average speed of rise varied between 0.1 percentage points for Rubber and Rubber Products and 159.87 percentage points for Jute Textiles of India, while in U.K. it varied from 16.07 percentage points for Food to 1722.10 percentage points for Ship Building and Marine Engineering.

(v) Average speed of fall ranged between 23.01 percentage points for Tobacco and 175.41 percentage points for Jute Textiles of India. Food industry of U.K. had lowest average speed of fall of 15.15 percentage points while Ship Building and Marine Engineering had largest, fall, 1786.14 percentage points over the study period.

(vi) Most of the industries of India and U.K. experienced high fluctuations in both, the rise and the fall.

(vii) Rubber and Rubber Products industry of India had smallest per year amplitude in rise (0.1 percentage point) and fall (4.39 percentage points) while Jute Textiles had largest per year rise (693.54 percentage points) and fall (674.78 percentage points).

Drink industry of U.K. had lowest per year amplitude in rice (8.81 percentage points) while Food had lowest fall (10.45 percentage points). Ship Building and Marine Engineering experienced largest per year amplitude in rise (1594.77 percentage points) as well as fall (965.37 percentage points during the 29 years' period).

(viii) 7 out of 19 Indian industries (36.8%)and 11 out of 17 U.K. industries (64.7%) had relatively less fluctuations in both the rise and fall. Thus, British manufacturing industries faced relatively stable profitability than Indian ones during the study period.

In sum, British manufacturing industries performed better than Indian ones over this period. Though the highest mean rate of profit for U.K. industries was relatively smaller than Indian ones, the former had relatively much less dispersion in their profitability series than the latter industries, revealing the stability in earning rates of U.K. industry compared to Indian industries.

As regards business cycles, though the phases of contraction and expansion numbered the same, the years covered under phases differed. Majority of industries had complete 5-6 TPT/PTP cycles while Basic and Capital Goods industries had complete 8-9 TPT/PTP cycles. Jute industry of India and Ship Building and Marine Engineering of U.K. are found to be highly fluctuation industries in terms of coefficient of variation, and speed of rise or fall, i.e., amplitude of business cycles.

Policy Implications

(A) Policy for India

The declining trend in profitability of 8 out of 19 (42.4%) Indian manufacturing industries studied here is a very big cause of concern. Though these industries belong to all the sectors, most of these are Basic and Capital Goods industries, or produce necessities of life. The falling tendency of profit rate of these industries is a proof of adverse effect of various controls on prices, output, expansion, investment, distribution, etc. exerted by government on these industries over time, consequently, these industries have lost their earnings capacity over time. Moreover, industries belonging to Basic and Capital Goods sector had to face the competitition from their public sector counterpart, as many of these industries are predominantly in the public sector.

If the country aims at speedy growth via industrialisation, the results of this study suggest that removal of all types of controls of manufacturing sector is the foremost step to be taken and, in that sense, the New Industrial Policy of 1991 is a step in right direction. The country needs increased competition which would enhance efficiency, productivity and profitability of industrial sector and the economy.

The results of mean value of profit rate, coefficient of variation and amplitude of business cycles have revealed that most of the Indian manufacturing industries (except few agro-based ones) studied here, underwent moderate fluctuations in their profit rates during the study period. However, most of the agro-based industries experienced very high fluctuations in profitability. These industries suffered from some type of controls of one hand, and faced problems like shortage of raw materials, power shortage, worn out machinery and techinques of production, etc. Obviously, these industries need immediate attention so that the supply of raw materials is assured. Since these industries depend upon agricultural sector and the government sector basic and heavy industries for the provision of raw materials, it is essential that working of both these sectors improves. This calls for modernisation of agricultural sector and raising of efficiency of public sector enterprises, production of Basic and Capital Goods. Again, this tempts us to advocate the policy of opening up of private and public sector for competition, both domestically and internationally, so that it would enhance efficiency, productivity and profitability of all the concerns in the manufacturing sector, and, in turn, of economy at large.

The results of the study on profitability trends and business cycles have revealed that majority of industries of manufacturing sector are prone to deviation cycles of short period of 2 to 3 years. However, it is further observed that agro-based industries, and those which belong to Basic, Capital and Intermediary Goods Sectors, suffered from very wide fluctuations, in both, the rise and fall of profitability, over the study period of 29 years. This confirms to the results derived earlier and induces us to strongly advocate the extension of the policy of liberalisation in the country. However, this is to be achieved with a minimum required combination of public enterprises, working efficiently, facing competition from private sector, and, retaining the philosophy of mixed economy.

(B) Policy for U.K.

U.K. experienced rising profitability in case of six industries, out of which 3 belonged to Consumer Goods Sector, while one industry from each of the Other 3 sectors had the rising trend in profit rate over the study period. This is well-come trend and needs to be further accentuated through proper policies by the government via enfusing competition and enhancing efficiency, productivity and profitability further, so that wide international marked is captured.

However, declining trend in profitability of majority of Capital Goods industries, viz., Vehicles, Metal Goods Not Elsewhere Specified and Ship Building and Marine Engineering, is big cause of concern. This may be attributable to lack of international competitiveness on account of wage increases in the industries, higher rates of inflation in U.K., low productivity, lack of investment of poor management. Jones and Cockerill (47, 1985) have observed, "Overall, about a quarter of the domestic market is held by imports, a proportion that has risen from 17 per cent is 1970. Penetration is particularly severe in instrument engineering (58%), Ship Building and marine Engineering (42%) and Vehicles (41%). "Thus import penetration, in U.K., though is not different from that in other European Community, it poses a significant threat to domestic manufactureres. Obviously, the thrust of the policy of U.K. should be on re-capturing some part of the home market lost to imports and to expand export sales, because, considerable scope exists for U.K. manufacturers to increase output, which, inturn, would enhancement employment, investment and profits.

Moreover, it has been observed that price elasticities of U.K.'s exports and imports are low. Hence, export demand does not rise much with a fall in price of exports. Since import demand in U.K. is often insensitive to price, exchance rate changes have little impact on earnings of manufacturing industries.

If we look at the figures of Index Number of Industrial Production at constant factor cost (1958=100), it is observed that for U.K.'s manufacturing sector it rose from 119.0 in 1963 to 168.6 in 1973, after which, it continuously declined to 138.7 in 1981. Similar trend is observed from total industrial production excluding Oil (See Jones and Cockerill, 47, 1985, p.85). These figures reveal the fact that production in manufacturing sector has declined greatly during the study period in U.K. Similar tendency is observed for all the 3 industries suffering from declining profitability.

Moreover, it has been observed that labour productivity in U.K. not only declined since 1963, but it was much below that of Japan, France West Germany and Italy. Jones and Cockerill (47,1985) observe that Output per person hour had an average annual increase of 5% in U.K. during 1963-68, while for Japan it was 15%, France, 6.6%, West Germancy 7.4%, Italy 9.2%, In 1979-82 it fell for U.K. to 2.4%, while for others to 1.2%, 1.8%, 0.8%, 2.7% respectively. In short, not only total output, but the rate of growth of labour productivity also declined greatly in U.K. between the period 1963-62.

It is further observed (Jones and Cockerill, 47, 1985, p.85 Table 5.1) that index number of production for U.K.'s industries experiencing rising profit rate over study period also showed a great increase between 1963-1981, e.g., it rose from 115.0 in 1963 to 151.6 in 1981 for Food, Drink and Tobacco, from 138.6 to 262.6 respectively for Chemicals and Allied Industries, from 132.6 to 225.1 respectively for Electrical Engineering, from 116.1 to 138.7 respectively for Paper, Printing and Publishing, and, from 141.0 to 225.8 respectively for Other Manufacturing Industries.

Thus, the major thrust of policy for improvement of earning capacity of manufacturing industries should be on increase in productivity and production, alongwith greater emphasis on increased competition, and efficiency, so that international competitiveness is generated and exports raised, while reducing the imports expanded home markets.

It is interesting to observe further that most of the British manufacturing industries underwent relatively less fluctuations during the study period, except some of capital goods industries mentioned above. These industries experienced longer complete 8-9 TPT/PTP cycles while other industries had complete 5-6 cycles. This is confirmed by the results on mean rate of profit, value of coefficient of variation and amplitude of business cycles.

In addition to above mentioned measures, there remain the problems of non-price factors in international competitiveness of U.K. manufacturing goods. These include improvement in quality design, reliability and after sale service, etc. Thus the policy prescription for U.K. manufacturing sector should include both type of measures, viz., traditional measure leading to competitive pricing and, non-price factors mentioned above, so that exports are promoted more and imports reduced via expansion of domestic markets.

In short, the proper policies need to be followed for each of the countries, with emphasis on increased competition, efficiency, productivity and profitability in both the countries. However, to retain the political and economic philosophies of India and U.K., the policy of liberalisation is advocated for the former, while for the latter, emphasis improvements on foreign trade is essential.

Areas for further Research

The study is concluded by indicating broadly some areas of further research in the related fields of comparative study undertaken here.

(i) The time trend analysis undertaken here is confined to the application of simple Linear Bivariate Time Trend model to the profitability of various manufacturing industries of India and U.K. For a better understanding of earnings trends of these industries, fittings of semi-log or log-log model or quadratic model would reveal the profitability trends more clearly for various industries and be more useful for policy framing.

(ii) The celebrated tendency of classical writers regarding equalising tendency of profit rates of various industries to tend to a certain value can be examined to throw light on the existence of the competitive conditions in two different type of economies.

(iii) Economic theory also assets a close relationship between the profitability of an industry, and, the use of monopoly power by large firms. Thus, an important area of further research is to explore the relationship between profitability and monopoly power, latter being expressed through concentration ratio. This would also help to understand the extent of imperfections prevailing in a mixed economy like India, and a competitive economy like U.K.

(iv) An examination of determinants of profitability in two countries with different environments would also throw very interesting results.

(v) For framing pricing policy, it would be interesting to arrive at the desired profit differentials between priority and non-priority industries, and within the priority industries, especially for India.

(vi) Looking at the differences in profitability of various manufacturing industries, it seems to be very interesting to examine the influence of risk differential on profitability and, the weightage that needs to be attached to it, so that, appropriate profitability differentials can be worked out.

(v) In order to examine whether strong positive tendency for the rates of profit to persist over short periods of 5 years, or, longer periods of decade's period, a test of persistency of rates of profit can be carried out. This would help us establish a casual functional relationship between past and present rates of profit.

(vii) A study on growth cycles by comparing the rate of growth of actual profit rate to that of its trend value, would help confirm the results drawn here.

(viii) Examination of profitability and growth relationship would help establish the casual relationship between growth of the industry and profitability.

Further research work in above mentioned areas would be of great practical significance and would throw more light on the operation of manufacturing sectors of two different types of economic systems, viz., India, and U.K.

Bibliography

Al Bhimani (1993) : "Performance measures in U.K. manufacturing companies : the state of play, *Management Accounting*, U.K., December, 1993, pp. 20–21.

Al Bhimani (1994) : "Monitoring Performance Measures in U.K. Manufacturing Companies, *Management Accounting*, U.K., January, 1994, pp. 36–37.

Asthana, B.N. (1972) : *Elements of Statistics*, Chaitanya Publishing House, Bombay, India, 1972.

Bain, J.S. (1951): "Relation of Profit Rates of Industry Concentraton in American Manufacturing 1936–1940, *Quarterly Journal of Economics*, August, 1951.

Bain, J.S. (1956) : *Barriers to New Competition, Their Character and Consequence in Manufacturing Industries*, Harvard University Press, Cambridge, Mass, 1956.

Barna, T. (1961) : "On Measuring Capital" in *The Theory of Capital*, eds. Lutz, F.A. and Hague, D.C., Macmillan, London, 1961.

Barna, T. (1962) : *Investment and Growth Policies in British Industrial Firms*, Cambridge University Press, Cambridge, U.K., 1962.

Berg, Elliot (1987) : "Privatisation : Developing a Pragmatic Approach," *Financial Express*, Ahmedabad, Gujarat, India, July 8, 1987.

Bhagawati, J.N. and Desai, P. (1970) : *India Planning for Industrialisation : Industrialisation and Trade Policies since 1951*. Oxford University Press, London, U.K., 1970.

Bagawati Jagdish (1988) : "Economic Performance : Objectives and Policy Design, and, "Economic Performance : Why Low Productivity ? ", *Economic Times*, February 10 and 11, 1988, Bombay, India.

B.M. (1987) : "Liberalisation of Economic Policies : World Bank's New Push," *Economic and Political Weekly*, Vol. XXII, Nos. 2–3, June 6, 1987, Bombay, India.

B.M. (1988) : "Privatisation, Indian Style," *Economic and Political Weekly*, Vol. XXII, No. 32, August 8, 1988, Bombay, India.

Bowan, R.T. (1934) : *Statistical Study of Profits*, Piladelphia, 1934.

Brahmanand, P.R. (1986) : "The Emerging Economic Framework, An Analysis of India's New Economic Policy," Forum of Free Enterprise, February, 1986, Bombay, India.

Burns, A.F. and Mitchell, W.C. (1946) : *Measuring Business Cycles*, N.B.E.R., New York, 1946.

Central Statistical Organisation : *National Accounts Statistics*, Various issues, C.S.O., Government of India, Calcutta, India.

Centre for Monitoring Indian Economy (1986) : *The Liberalisation Process, Indian Economy*, CMIE, July, 1986, Bombay, India.

Chitre, V.C. (1982) : "Growth Cycles in Indian Economy," *Artha Vijnana*, Vol. 24, No. 4, December, 1982, Pune, India.

Correspondent, The Economic Times (1991) : "The NIP : Challenges and Opportunities," *The Economic Times* (midweek review), August 22, 1991, Ahmedabad, Gujarat, India.

Denison, E.F. (1967) : *Why Growth Rates Differ?* Washington, The Brookings Institution, U.S.A., 1967.

Dudic, T.S. (1975) : *How to Improve Profitability Through More Effective Planning*, John Wiley and Sons, New York, U.S.A., 1975.

Dutt, R.C. (1991) : "The Industrial Policy," *Mainstream*, Vol. XXIX, No. 43, August 17, 1991, India.

Eatwell, J.L. (1971) : "Growth, Profitability and Size : The Empirical Evidence," in *The Corporate Economy*, Marris, R. and Wood, A (eds.), Macmillan, London, U.K., 1971.

Economic and Scientific Research Foundation (1964) : *Guide To Performance of Top 200 Companies*, E.S.R.F., 1964, New Delhi, India.

Economic and Scientific Research Foundation (1970) : Top 300 Companies, E.S.R.F., 1970, New Delhi, India.

Editorial Article (1991) : "Labour Friendly Too," *The Times of India*, July 27, 1991, Ahmedabad, Gujarat, India.

Epstein, E.I. and Gordon, R.A. (1939) : "Profits of Selected American Industrial Corporations," *The Review of Economics and Statistics*, August, 1939.

Epstein, R.C. (1934) : *Industrial Profits in United States*, National Bureau of Economic Research, New York, U.S.A., 1934.

Financial Express (1991) : "Text of Industrial Policy : Liberalisation for Rapid Growth," *Financial Express*, July, 25, 1991, Bombay, India.

Foulke, R.A. (1966) : *Practical Financial Statement Analysis*, Tata McGraw-Hill Pub. Co. Ltd., Bombay, India, 1966.

Friedman, M. and Schwartz, A. : "Money and Business Cycles," *Review of Economics and Statistics*, Vol. 45, No. 1, Part 2 : Supplement.

Fuchs, V.R. (1961) : "Integration, Concentration and Profits in Manufacturing Industries," *Quarterly Journal of Economics*, February, 1961.

George, K.D. (1968) : "Concentration, Barrier to Entry and Rate of Return," *Review of Economics and Statistics*, May, 1968.

Ghosh, Arun (1987) : "Liberalisation, Competition and Import Policy," *Economic and Political Weekly*, Vol. XXII, No. 26, June 27, 1987.

Ghosh, Arun (1991) : "The Left : Neither Wrong, Nor to Blame," *The Economic Times*, October 2, 1992, Ahmedabad, Gujarat, India.

Gujarati, Damodar (1978) : *Basic Econometrics*, McGraw-Hill Book Co., 1978, New York, U.S.A.

Gupta, L.N. (1977) : *A Study into the Profitability of Government Companies : With Reference to Selected Running Concerns*, Oxford and I.B.H. Publishing Company, 1977, New Delhi, India.

Guthman, H.G. (1968) : *Analysis of Financial Statements*, Prentice Hall of India Pvt. Ltd., 1968, New Delhi, India.

Hart, P.E. (1965, 1968) : *Studies in Profit, Business Saving and Investment in the United Kingdom, 1920–62*, Vols. I and II, George Allen and Unwin Ltd., 1965, 1968, London, U.K.

Henderson, R.F. and Tew, B. (1959) : *Studies in Company Finance*, Cambridge University Press, Cambridge, 1959, U.K.

H.M.S.O. (1979–90) : *Business Monitor, Company Finance*, Various Issues, H.M.S.O., London, U.K.

Indian Council of Social Sciences Research (1975) : *Survey of Research in Economics* : Vol. 5, I.C.S.S.R., Government of India, 1975, New Delhi, India.

Industrial Credit and Investment Corporation of India Ltd. (1977) : *Financial Performance of Companies*, Portfolio 1975–76, ICICI, 1977, Bombay, India.

Iyer Ramaswamy, R. (1988) : "The Privatisation Argument," *Economic and Political Weekly*, Vol. XXII, No. 11, March 12, 1988, Bombay, India.

Jhaveri, N.J. (1991) : "Privatisation : The Nuts and Bolts Issues," *The Economic Times*, September 24, 1991, Ahmedabad, Gujarat, India.

Johnston, J. (1972) : *Econometric Methods*, McGraw-Hill, Koga Kusha Ltd., 1972, Tokyo, Japan.

Jones, T.T. and Cockerill, T.A.J. (1985) : *Structure and Performance of Industries*, Heritage Publishers, 1985, New Delhi, India.

Jones, W.T. (1969) : *Size, Growth and Profitability in Mechanical Engineering Industry* (Unpublished), National Economic Development Office, 1969, London, U.K.

Krishnaswamy, K.S. (1991) : "On Liberalisation and some Related Matters," *Economic and Political Weekly*, Vol. XXVI, No. 42, October 19, 1991, Bombay, India.

Kuchhal, S.C. (1973) : *Corporate Finance, Principles and Problems*, Chaitanya Publishing House, 1973, Allahabad, U.P., India.

Kuchhal, S.C. (1978) : *Industrial Economy of India*, Chaitanya Publishing House, 1978, Allahabad, U.P., India.

Kmenta, Jan. (1971) : *Elements of Econometrics*, The Macmillan Company, 1971, London, U.K.

Lakdawala, D.T. (1991) : "New Policy Measures," *Economic and Political Weekly*, Vol. XXVI, No. 34, August 24, 1991, Bombay, India.

Marris, R.L. (1964) : *Income Policy and the Rate of Profit in Industry* : Proceeding of the Manchester Statistical Society, December, 1964, U.K.

Marris, R.L. (1967) : "Profitability and Growth in Industrial Firm," *Business Ratios*, Spring, 1967.

Marris, R.L. and Wood, A. (1964) : *The Corporate Economy : Growth, Competition and Innovative Potential*, Macmillan and Company, 1964, London, U.K.

Mehta, B.V. (1961) : *Industrial Profits in India* (Unpublished Ph.D. Thesis), Bombay University, 1961, Bombay, India.

Ministry of Information and Broadcasting (1991) : *New Industrial Policy*, August 8, 1991, Government of India, New Delhi, India.

Mintz, I. (1969) : *Dating Post-war Business Cycles : Methods and Their Application to Western Germany 1950–67*, N.B.E.R., 1969, New York, U.S.A.

Mintz, I. (1974) : *Dating, United States Growth Cycles, Explorations in Economic Research*, Vol. I, No. 1. N.B.E.R., 1974, New York, U.S.A.

Misra, S.K. and Puri, V.K. (1991) : *Indian Economy*, Himalaya Publishing House, 1991, Bombay, India.

Mong, G.S. (1975) : *Mathematics and Statistics for Economics*, Vikas Publishing House Pvt. Ltd., 1975, New Delhi, India.

Morgn, D.R. and England, R.E. (1988) : "The Two Faces of Privatisation," *Public Administrative Review*, Nov. 1988.

Mukhopadhyay, J.K. (1988) : *The Privatisation Phenomenon and Its Relevance to Developing Countires*, Forum of Free Enterprise, July, 1988, Bombay, India.

Nagar, A.L. and Das, R.K. (1976) : *Basic Statistics*, Oxford University Press, 1976, Delhi, India.

Pandey, D.P. (1975) : *Size Profitability and Growth : A Study of Indian Industry* (Unpublished Ph.D. Thesis), Bombay University, 1975, Bombay, India.

Pani Narendra (1991) : "Need for Wider Structural Adjustment," *The Economic Times*, October, 18, 1991, Ahmedabad, Gujarat, India.

Patel, I.G. (1986) : "New Economic Policy," *The Economic Times*, November 6–8, 1986, Ahmedabad, Gujarat, India.

Paranjape, H.K. (1977) : "Industrial Growth with Justice—India's Strategy," *Some Problems of India's Economic Policy*, edited by Wadhava, C.D.

Paranjape, H. K. (1991) : "New Industrial Policy : A Capitalist Manifesto," *Economic and Political Weekly*, Vol. XXVI, No. 43, October 26, 1991, Bombay, India.

Parker, J.E.S. (1964) : "Profitability and Growth of British Industrial Firms," *Manchester School of Economics and Social Studies*, May, 1964, U.K.

Paul Samuel (1988) : "Privatisation : A Review of International Experience," *Economic and Political Weekly*, Vol. XXIII, No. 6, February 6, 1988, Bombay, India.

Pendse, D.R. (1985) : *Privatisation and Economic Growth*, Forum of Free Enterprise, June, 1985, Bombay, India.

Penrose, E.T. (1955) : "Limits to Growth and Size of the Firms," *American Economic Review*, Vol. 45, 1955, U.S.A.

Penrose, E.T. : *The Theory of Growth of Firms*, Basic Blackwell.

Raj, K.N. (1985) : *New Economic Policy*, V.T. Krishnammachari Memorial Lecture, 1985, Oxford University Press, Bombay, India.

Rede, L.A. (1981) : "Structural Changes of Rate of Profit in Indian Manufacturing Industries," *Productivity*, Vol. XXII, No. 1, April–June, 1981, National Productivity Council (NPC), New Delhi, India.

Rede, L.A. (1983) : "Towards Profitability of Manufacturing Industries," *Productivity*, January–March, 1983, Vol. XXIII, No. 4, N.P.C., New Delhi, India.

Rede, L.A. (1984) : *Structure of Profit Rates in Indian Manufacturing Industries*, R.B.E., Baroda, 1984, Gujarat.

Rede, L.A. (1987) : "Scope for Privatisation in India through Diverstiture and Denationalisation," *Asian Journal of Economics and Social Studies*, Vol. 6, No. 3, July, 1987, Muzaffarnagar, India.

Rede, L.A. (1988) : "Business Cycles and Rate of Profit in Indian Manufacturing Industries : 1950–51 to 1977–78," *Artha-Vijnana*, Vol. 30, No. 3, September, 1988, Gokhale Institute of Politics and Economics, Pune, Maharastra, India.

Rede, L.A. (1989) : "PRIVATISATION : Institutional Approach," *The Economic Times*, April 22, 1989, Bombay, India.

Rede, L.A. (1991) : "RESTRUCTURING OF STATE OWNED ENTERPRISES (SOEs)," *Commerce and Management*, December, 1991, Muzaffarnagar, India.

Rede, L.A. (1992) : "INDIA'S NEW INDUSTRIAL POLICY : A VIEW," *The Asian Economic Review*, Indian Institute of Economics, Hyderabad, April, 1992, A.P., India.

Reserve Bank of India (1975) : *Financial Statistics of Joint Stock Companies in India, 1960–61 to 1970–71*, R.B.I., August, 1975, Bombay, India.

Reserve Bank of India (1977) : *Financial Statistics of Joint Stock Companies in India, 1970–71 to 1974–75*, R.B.I., August, 1977, Bombay, India.

Reserve Bank of India (1975 to 1981) : *Finances of Medium and Large Public Limited Companies in India*, Various Issues of R.B.I. Bulletins for 1975–1981, R.B.I., Bombay, India.

Reserve Bank of India (1981–88) : *Finances of Medium and Large Public Limited Companies in India*, Computer Print Out, R.B.I., Bombay, India.

Rosen, G. (1958) : *Industrial Change in India : Industrial Growth, Capital Requirement and Technological Change, 1937–1955*, Free Press, 1958, Illinois, U.S.A.

Sandesara, J.C. (1987) : "Privatisation : The Wheel is Turning," *The Economic Times*, November 30, 1987, Bombay, India.

Sandesara, J.C. (1991) : "Higher Growth Round The Corner (Midweek Review)," *The Economic Times*, August 22, 1991, Ahmedabad, Gujarat, India.

Sandesara, J.C. (1991) : "New Industrial Policy : Questions of Efficient Growth and Social Objectives," *Economic and Political Weekly*, Vol. XXVI, Nos. 31 and 32, August 3–10, 1991, Bombay, India.

Segura, Edilberto (1988) : "Industrial, Trade and Financial Sector Policies to Foster Private Enterprises in Developing Countries, "*The Columbia Journal of World Business*, Spring, 1988, Columbia, U.S.A.

Sherman, H.J. (1968) : *Profits in the United States*, Cornell University Press, 1968, Ithaca, New York, U.S.A.

Shroff, Manu (1988) : "Economic Policy Issues," *The Economic Times*, April 13–14, 1988, Bombay, India.

Singh, A. and Whittington, G. (1968) : *Growth, Profitability and Valuation*, Cambridge University Press, 1968, Cambridge, U.K.

Singh, A. and Whittington, G. (1970) : *Growth, Profitability and Valuation : A Note*, Dept. of Applied Economics, Mimeo, Cambridge University, Cambridge, 1970.

Stigler, G.J. (1963) : *Capital and Rate of Return in Manufacturing Industries*, Princeton University Press, 1963, Princeton, U.S.A.

Stockton, J.R. and Clark, C.T. (1972) : *Introduction To Business and Economic Statistics*, D.B. Taraporwala and Sons and Co. Pvt. Ltd., 1972, Bombay, India.

Subrahmaniam, K.K. and Papola, T.S. (1971) : "Profitability and Growth of Indian Chemicals Industry," *Anveshak*, Vol. I, June, 1971, S.P.I., Ahmedabad, Gujarat, India.

Summers, H.B. (1932) : "A Comparison of the Rates of Earnings in Large Scale Industries," *Quarterly Journal of Economics*, Vol. 41, 1931–32.

Tendulkar, Suresh (1991) : "Economic Reform : Hostage of Interest Groups," *The Economic Times*, September 17, 1991, Bombay, India.

Tandon, Prakash (1984) : "A New Design for India's Public Sector," Mohan Mangalam Memorial Lecture, 1984, Staff College, Hyderabad, A.P., India.

Tandon, Prakash (1984) : "Public Sector : A Different Angle," Nehru Commemorative Lecture, Documentation Centre for Corporate and Business Policy Research and Scope, August 30, 1984, Delhi, India.

Trivedi, M.L. (1986) : *Government and Business*, Multi-tech Publishing Company, 1986, Bombay, India.

Twentieth Century Fund (1937) : *How Profitable Is a Big Business* ?, The I.C.F., 1937, New York, U.S.A.

Wadhava, Charan D. (ed.) (1977) : *Some Problems of India's Economic Policy*, Tata McGraw-Hill Pub. Co. Ltd., 1977, Bombay, India.

Wadhava, C.D. (1987) : "Economic Policy—Some Imperatives," *Financial Express*, September 2, 1987, Bombay, India.

Waters, A.R. (1987) : "The Technique of Privatisation," Excerpts from Privatisation : A Viable Policy Option," in *Enterpreneurship and Privatising of Government*, Calvin A. Kent (eds.), 1987.

Whittington, G. (1971) : The Prediction of Profitability, Cambridge University Press, 1971, Cambridge, U.K.

Index